# LEADING LEGENDS

**Female Superintendents Breaking Barriers with Purpose and Power**

*Myrna Rivera Côté*

*Lillian Maldonado French*

*Lisbeth Johnson*

*Linda Kimble*

*Martha Martinez*

*Cindy Petersen*

*Carol Riley*

*Marilou Ryder*

*Patricia Clark White*

*Marylou Wilson*

LEADING LEGENDS: Female Superintendents Breaking Barriers with Purpose and Power

©2025 Myrna Rivera Côté, Lillian Maldonado French, Lisbeth Johnson, Linda Kimble ,Martha Martinez, Cindy Petersen, Carol Riley, Marilou Ryder, Patricia Clark White, Marylou Wilson

All rights reserved: No part of this publication may be reproduced or transmitted in any form or by any means, mechanical or electronic, including photocopying and recording or by information storage and retrieval system without permission in writing from the authors (except by a reviewer, who may quote brief passages).

ISBN: 979-8-9927034-1-2

Epub: 979-8-9927034-2-9

Library of Congress Control Number 2025940054

Disclaimer: The Publisher and Authors have made every effort to ensure the information in this anthology is accurate, timely, and valuable. However, given the ever-evolving nature of the world, some content may change over time. The insights and advice shared reflect personal experiences and perspectives, which may not apply universally to all readers or situations.

This anthology is provided with the understanding that the Publisher and Authors are not offering legal, medical, or other professional advice. No guarantees are made regarding specific outcomes, and neither the Publisher nor the Authors shall be held liable for any loss, damage, or inconvenience resulting from the use of the information presented.

References to organizations or websites do not imply endorsement. Please be aware that links or references may no longer be active or accurate at the time of reading.

To respect privacy, names and identifying details have been changed where appropriate.

Printed in the United States of America

Delmar Publishing, Huntington Beach, CA 92648

**Publicity Rights**

For Information on publicity, author interviews, presentation, and subsidiary rights, contact:

Dr. Marilou Ryder: drmlr@yahoo.com 760-900-0556

# Contents

| | | |
|---|---|---|
| *Foreword* | | ii |
| *Preface* | | xi |
| *Introduction* | | xii |
| I. | Women in Power | 1 |
| II. | Leading Out Loud | 14 |
| III. | The Days are Long, But the Years are Short | 27 |
| IV. | First Woman Ever | 35 |
| V. | Leading Through the Storm | 42 |
| VI. | The Unlikely Candidate | 53 |
| VII. | Grace Under Fire | 61 |
| VIII. | The Day the Dead Guy Drove to School | 77 |
| IX. | Whiplash Territory | 91 |
| X. | Trust Your Gut | 100 |
| XI. | Opening Doors | 107 |
| XII. | Built From the Ground Up | 118 |
| XIII. | When It's Time to Leave | 135 |
| XIV. | Bold Enough to Believe | 141 |
| *References* | | 147 |
| *About the Authors* | | 151 |

# VOICES *OF* POWER

Be willing to dream beyond what others say cannot be done.

# Foreword

The stories in **Leading Legends** shed light on the quiet strength and resilience of retired superintendents—women who helped redefine what leadership can look like in education. They didn't seek recognition, but their efforts cracked ceilings, opened doors, and paved the way for others to follow. By sharing their stories, they hope to pass on the lessons they've learned and encourage the next generation of women to lead with courage and purpose.

But we didn't want to stop there. To bring this legacy full circle, we reached out to current superintendents, women who are leading in real-time. We asked them to share a truth, a lesson, or a piece of hard-earned advice from their own leadership journey. What emerged is more than a traditional foreword—it's a living conversation between generations.

Together, these voices —those who paved the way and those still walking it —create a powerful chorus of insight, strength, and solidarity. Whether you're already in a top role or just beginning to imagine yourself there, may their words remind you that you're not alone and your leadership matters.

One truth I've learned as a female superintendent is that authenticity is your greatest strength. You don't have to mimic others to lead well—your voice, perspective, and leadership style are powerful just as they are. Leading with empathy, integrity, and confidence creates real impact. Trust yourself, even when others question you. You've earned your seat at the table—own it fully.

**Dr. Roxane Fuentes**
**Superintendent**
**Berryessa Union School District**

Enough cannot be said about surrounding yourself with highly effective leaders who are learners, critical thinkers, and who prioritize students above all else. When I've hired well and continue to support these highly effective people, every aspect of my career and my home life has fallen into place. As a female leader, wife, and mother, my responsibilities can feel overwhelming at times. However, as I've continued to develop my leadership team and hired LEADERS, the responsibility juggle feels less like a juggle and more like a phenomenally executed balancing act. Bottom line, surround yourself with leaders, leaders who care about what you believe is important and support these people well.

**Dr. Kristin Baranski**
**Superintendent**
**Santee School District**

One truth I've learned as a female superintendent is that navigating the political landscape of educational leadership demands fortitude, listening deeply and speaking clearly, and intentionally cultivating relationships and networks. Politics are a reality; approach them strategically, leveraging your abilities to build consensus, foster collaboration, and remain true to your core values. Your authenticity, tempered by political savvy, is your greatest asset. Embrace it fully and lead boldly.

**Dr. Leisa Winston**
**Superintendent**
**Huntington Beach City School District**

This book, a testament to the groundbreaking leadership of retired female superintendents, unveils the power of courage, strategic thinking, and heartfelt dedication in shattering barriers within education. Their journeys offer invaluable insights for all aspiring and current female leaders. From my own experiences as a superintendent, one truth has resonated deeply: leading as a woman requires an unwavering commitment to *integrity* in every action, the intentional cultivation of authentic and *supportive relationships*, and the development of a *strong back* to stand firm in your convictions, all while leading with a *soft heart* that centers compassion and connection. Embrace your unique strengths, connect with inspirational superstars who are doing the same work, and never underestimate the transformative impact of leading with both conviction and care. May their stories and this truth inspire you to lead with your whole self and create lasting change for kids!

**Dr. Kimberly McGrath**
**Superintendent**
**Reed Union School District**

I have been honored to deepen my leadership and expand my influence in service to students, teachers, staff, and the broader community over many years. At the heart of my leadership philosophy is a clear understanding that the role of the superintendent is not simply to lead from the front but to serve — to ensure that every voice is heard and every perspective is valued as we move our work forward.

I am deeply committed to ensuring that all students have equitable access to education and meaningful opportunities to thrive. Public education is, by its nature, diverse — and our effectiveness as educators grows when we take the time to listen, learn, and lead alongside the many voices and cultures that make up our district community. As a female superintendent in a space that has historically been a male-dominated space, I have come to deeply appreciate the importance of taking a seat at the table — not only for myself, but for all those I represent. It is essential to know you belong, to use your voice with confidence, and to trust that your lived experiences and insights have the power to shape conversations and decisions for the better. Representation matters—and with it comes both responsibility and opportunity.

**Sara Noguchi, Ed.D.**
**Superintendent**
**Modesto City Schools**

As a woman leader situated in the top spot in a school district, you will constantly need to remind yourself that you are more than qualified to be in this esteemed position. It is true that as a woman, performance expectations are raised higher for you than for a man. You might need to remind your board members of this reality. Speak up with confidence always.

**Dr. Tracy Smith**
**Superintendent**
**Novato Unified School District**

One truth I've learned is the critical importance of self-advocacy and confidently articulating your vision, even when it challenges the status quo. As women, we may sometimes be socialized to prioritize collaboration over asserting our own perspectives, but the superintendency demands both. You must be prepared to clearly and consistently communicate your goals, defend your decisions with conviction, and ensure your voice is heard at every table. The work of a superintendent is challenging, even more so as a female superintendent. Finding your

village and forming a supportive circle that can be there for you to celebrate and also lift you up is critical. This assertiveness, grounded in your expertise and values, is not only essential for effective leadership but also for paving the way for other women in education.
**Dr. Holly Edds**
**Superintendent**
**Orcutt Union School District**

Throughout my career as an educator and now as a superintendent, one of the most impactful truths I've learned is the importance of leading with authenticity. It is essential to have clarity about your core values—what you believe in and stand for. These beliefs guide your decisions and actions. Ultimately, it is your actions rooted in these values that define your leadership and earn the trust of others.
**Dr. Lucy Van Scyoc**
**Superintendent**
**Tulare Joint Union High School District**

One truth I've learned about leading as a woman superintendent is that the higher you rise, the more visible and vulnerable you become—and with that comes both great responsibility and profound opportunity. The scrutiny can be intense, but it also opens the door to lead boldly and model what inclusive, values-driven leadership looks like. I've learned that leading with empathy doesn't diminish your strength; it enhances your impact and deepens your connection to those you serve. Making student-centered decisions, even when they are difficult or unpopular, keeps you grounded in purpose and reminds you why this work matters. When you stay anchored in your values, lead with authenticity, and create space for others to lead beside you, not behind you, you cultivate a community built on trust, resilience, and shared vision. And in doing so, you not only navigate challenges but also help others rise and lead.

**Dr. Daisy Morales**
**Superintendent**
**Santa Rosa City Schools**

The journey of a female superintendent and true leadership begins with believing deeply in your own voice and vision. This Truth proves that challenges are not roadblocks but powerful opportunities to rise, adapt, and shine even brighter. Successful women leaders know that courage isn't the absence of fear — it's the decision to move forward anyway, fueled by purpose. We remind aspiring leaders that lifting others as you climb creates unstoppable momentum and lasting change. Most importantly, I have learned that dreaming boldly and leading fearlessly with a "Students First" vision isn't just possible—it's necessary.

**Gunn Marie Hansen, Ph.D**
**Superintendent**
**Westminster School District**

I hold deep respect and gratitude for the trailblazing sisterhood of retired female superintendents who paved the way for those of us who followed. Despite their legacy, the role of a female superintendent can still feel isolating. In a profession historically dominated by men, a self-perpetuating cycle persists in which superintendent roles often favor male candidates—even as women comprise the majority of the educational workforce.

To my current and aspiring female colleagues: remain grounded in your "why," and cultivate a strong professional support network. Your "why"—the core purpose that drives your passion for education—will sustain you through adversity and guide your pursuit of transformational change. It will keep your focus firmly on doing what is best for students and will serve as a compass in your leadership journey.

Equally important is building a network of fellow female superintendents. Regularly connecting with this community creates a trusted space for mentorship, shared learning, and mutual empowerment—fostering the collective strength needed to lead with courage and continue shaping the future of education.

**Dr. Rachel Valenzuela**
**Superintendent**
**Mark West Union School District**

# LEGACY TRUTHS

The loudest voices aren't always the wisest — listen carefully.

## Preface

Storytelling is one of the oldest forms of connection, a way for one voice to reach many across time and space. When we began this project, our goal was to capture the heart behind the titles, the trials behind the triumphs, and the truth behind the journeys of retired women superintendents who paved the way for others.

What unfolded was more than a collection of stories. It became a living legacy.

Each woman featured in this book has held one of the most demanding and influential roles in education, and yet, their stories are not just about leadership. They are about courage, conviction, resilience, and the often unspoken challenges of being a woman in a role still shaped by male-dominated expectations.

In today's world, where more women are stepping up and stepping into educational leadership, these narratives matter more than ever. Storytelling, when done honestly, does more than inspire, it equips. It lifts. It teaches. It reminds us we are not alone.

We hope that this book serves as both a mirror and a guidepost: a mirror that reflects the lived experiences of women who have led with integrity and vision and a guidepost for current and future leaders to lead with purpose and impact.

To every woman aspiring to the superintendency, may you find yourself in these pages — your ambition, your voice, and your power.

## INTRODUCTION

I recently received a text from a former doctoral student, now serving as an assistant superintendent: "Dr. Ryder, did you hear? Another female superintendent was just let go by the board. That makes three in the last six months."

That message, like many before it, lingered with me, a reflection of the hard truth that for women in leadership, earning the position is often just the beginning of the uphill battle to keep it.

As a university professor and chair of the Organizational Leadership Program, I serve as a study advisor to doctoral candidates as they research and write their dissertations. While I support students exploring a variety of topics, many of my female students choose to focus on the unique challenges faced by women in educational leadership.

Almost every dissertation includes the same disheartening statistics about how challenging it still is for women to rise and remain in top educational leadership roles. And nearly all of them reference Eliza Flagg. Mine did too, over twenty years ago.

> *Eliza Flagg was one of the earliest known female school superintendents in the U.S., appointed in 1857 in New York. Despite her groundbreaking role over 160 years ago, the percentage of women in superintendent positions remains disproportionately low. In many ways, the barriers she faced still exist—political scrutiny, gender bias, and job insecurity continue to challenge today's women leaders in education (Blount, 1998).*[1]

Then come the grim statistics.

*Women comprised just 9% of superintendents in 1910. By 1930, the number had risen slightly to 11%, but it fell again in 1950, and by 1971, it had reached a low of just 13%. Fast forward to 2025— after all the advocacy and effort— women still hold only 28% of superintendent roles (American Association of School Administrators (2025).*[2]

Now, contrast that with the teaching force. In 1999, 75% of teachers were women. By the 2020–21 school year, this figure had increased to 77%. While more recent data for 2025 is not yet available, the trend suggests a gradual increase in the proportion of female teachers over time (National Center for Education Statistics, 2023).[3]

The disparity is glaring. But here's the truth— despite the odds, women persist. We persist in climbing the ladder to become school superintendents, often with little guidance and even less support. Along the way, we learn to overcome self-sabotage, master effective communication, build our personal brands, and conquer our fears. We apply for a job, get it, and then show up on day one, only to suffer through Impostor Syndrome.

I remember my first day as superintendent. I picked up the phone and called my mentor, one of the women featured in this book.

"Hi," I said, "I'm sitting at my desk here in Fresno County. Two of my assistant superintendents wanted this job, and they've made it clear they're not happy I got it. Honestly, I feel like I landed this job by fluke."

She laughed gently and said, "Any chance you're wearing a black suit?"

"Of course," I replied.

"Then get up from your desk, walk around the district, meet people, and act like you've been doing this for years. Before long, you'll believe it yourself."

It worked—at least for a while.

Eventually, the Impostor Syndrome faded, but the real work began. The man who once held my job made it clear he wasn't exactly cheering for my success. During the search process, he openly lobbied the board to hire his assistant superintendent. This local favorite was married to the high school football coach, whose father had just happened to have the district's new stadium named after him. His message was loud and clear: I didn't belong here, and they picked the wrong woman.

Then came the surprise: "Our new football stadium will open at Homecoming," the board told me—in September. It was July. A quick visit to the site revealed that the stadium was nowhere near finished—at least a year behind schedule. Someone had overlooked a rather significant detail that no one had ever mentioned. The board was upset and seemed to think this oversight was my fault.

On my second day on the job, the new HR director visited me. He'd been promoted by the previous superintendent from middle school principal to Human Resource Director just before I arrived. In fact, the outgoing superintendent had filled nearly every cabinet-level position in the weeks leading up to my start.

This man sat in my office for nearly two hours—his version of a welcome was a warning. "They don't hire outsiders here," he said. "You're going to have to learn the Central Valley way."

On day three, a Saturday, I was alone in my rental home. My husband wouldn't be joining me for a few more weeks as we relocate from Huntington Beach to Fresno—quite a transition. I didn't know anyone in Fresno County and had no connection with the educational community.

Then the doorbell rang.

A young woman stood there, holding a foil-covered plate of cookies.

"Hi," she said. "I'm Sumer, the assistant principal at Riverbluff Elementary School. I live two streets over. I heard you just moved in and thought you might like a hand."

Startled but touched, I invited her in.

We talked. I mentioned how hard it was adjusting to the heat and how much I missed the coastal breeze. I asked Sumer if she could look at my wardrobe and help me find something more Central Valley-friendly. She immediately gained my trust—not because of anything grand, but because of her smile, the cookies, and the genuine way she seemed to care about my success.

She told me she was thrilled that I was the first female superintendent in the district. She was excited to work for a woman leader. Oh, I liked her already. She was a kindred spirit, sharing a belief in lifting women up.

That moment has stayed with me for over a decade.

She reminded me that we are never truly alone—not when we stand in solidarity.

Solidarity among women is both strength and strategy. When we rise together, we stay standing.

So here's the sobering truth—despite decades of advocacy, the percentage of female superintendents has barely budged in over 100 years.

And yet,

We persist.

We show up to one another's homes with cookies.

We take phone calls from women who feel like they got the job by accident.

We write books about how to get the job, how to stay in the job, and how to want the job—even when we doubt ourselves.

We lift each other up. That's how we do it.

This book is for every woman who's thinking about leadership. Maybe you're one of the 83% of female teachers ready for the next step. Perhaps you're a principal eyeing the superintendency. Or maybe you're already in the chair, trying to survive the whirlwind.

If even one story in this book makes your journey easier, we've done our job.

Packed with real talk, practical advice, and hard-earned wisdom, this book offers mentorship through the voices of retired superintendents. We're storytellers, yes, but more importantly, we're mentors who've lived it, led it, and learned from it. Think of this book as a fireside chat, a field guide, a blueprint for success.

And maybe—just maybe—the stories you find here will be the "cookies" of encouragement you didn't even know you needed.

**Dr. Marilou Ryder**

**Author, Professor, Editor**

Breaking barriers starts with breaking silence.

# Chapter I

## WOMEN IN POWER

### Dr. Lisbeth Johnson

The story I am about to share with you underscores the experiences I encountered during my decade-long tenure as the CEO of a school district. I have often experienced disbelief regarding males who, upon learning about my position, would respond with: "Well, how did you like being a teacher?" Downgrading a woman's role still permeates. The view that women are unable to manage CEO positions and successfully navigate critical organizational leadership roles remains a predominant perception in organizations.

For decades, companies denied women the opportunity for CEO positions. Those fortunate enough to land the CEO role need essential tools for success. Grit, a focus on engaging people, and strategic approaches, rather than ego-driven tactics, are the tools I used to chart my success as a leader. By the end of this story, I hope to inspire you to believe that you can persevere as a woman in a position of power and navigate uncharted waters, becoming a forceful decision-maker who purposefully steers your organization ship to shore.

**Small Town Politics**

Times have not changed much in the power structure between women and men in the 21st century. Urban politics typically follow traditional practices. Small towns often have strong, fixed beliefs about who holds power and who gets to enjoy privileges. Most of all, longtime residents strictly enforce the unspoken codes of behavior for how strangers and new residents are treated. Until they grant permission and the town's sages give the subtle "nod" they treat newcomers like undocumented outsiders. These newcomers are certainly not privy to what makes the town tick or where to find its societal keys or treasured secrets. For females, the doors to power in new communities can be difficult to access.

Such was the culture I voluntarily entered in the early 2000s by accepting a noteworthy position in a century-old school district in Santee, California. Santee, albeit recently modernized, still prides itself on its blue-collar ethics. In a suburb east of the mother metropolis of San Diego, nepotism, as well as male privilege, are alive and well in the Santee community. I encountered obstacles upon my arrival. Several of the elected officials attended school in the district during their youth. All the district Board members at the time had been long-time residents of Santee, and the City Council was governed by a good ole' boys' network of gentlemen who had ruled the town for decades. Elections did not upset the political order. The same political faces held offices year after year and election after election.

Santee had approximately 45,000 residents when I started my job. At the time, residents were mainly of Caucasian heritage, with families holding middle-class and blue-collar employment positions. The community boasted a healthy number of Christian churches per capita compared with any other small town in the county. The city was known by those who loved it as a wonderful place to raise a family; however, the sheriff's department could attest to another reputation—Santee was once dubbed the methamphetamine capital of the county. In addition, people of color often negatively referred to Santee as Clan Tee because of a Black soldier's murder in the town.

Yet, in this double identity culture of Santee, I was elated when I interviewed for a position to oversee the Educational Services Department and become a member of the Superintendent's Cabinet, a role highly touted for its accountability for student learning.

**Skills and Aspirations**

Upon my employment, I was eager to take on this role. I brought unique and much-needed skills to a small-town district like Santee. Nonetheless, it seemed to me and others that I was a trophy hire. I was one of the few people of color in leadership there. In fact, out of nearly two hundred employees in the school district, only four were people of color.

Santee was overall a very friendly town, despite some of the stories about its reputation in East San Diego County. I thrived there, not only because of my technical skills on the job but also because of my ability to collaborate with people and build a satisfying and effective team at the Santee School District. The days were grueling. However, since students achieved and our achievement steadily progressed, we eventually ranked eighth in student learning achievement among forty-two school districts in the county. By partnering with my direct reports in the department and leveraging our combined skill sets, I established a strong reputation in my role.

The School Board members were happy with my performance and the staff and I connected quite well. I loved working with people, regardless of their culture or background. While I started as an outsider, the Santee School District became a part of my family, and they welcomed me into their community as well.

Due to my efforts, I received a lifetime offer after about two years on the job. The Board unanimously voted to appoint me as Superintendent of Santee School District, overseeing 10 schools and serving 8,000 students. It was an incredible accomplishment—one that filled me with pride. I was also honored to be the first person of color to hold a top leadership position in the city's history, a milestone that carried deep personal significance.

Being superintendent was a thrilling adventure for me in a small town. I strived tirelessly to be successful in a role I had never expected to have in my lifetime. The School Board—political, like most boards—was, at the time of my hire, composed of five women from Santee. Some of the Board members had graced the school district's governance role for several years. It was clear that they wanted me to succeed. While we did not always agree on everything, I appreciated their authentic care and concern for the children and families of Santee. I respected the Board members because they had no unethical ulterior motives in conducting their governance duties. They also treated me as one of them, creating a valuable leadership partnership among us.

## Superintendent Challenges

Being a superintendent in a school district is a balancing act. Many superintendents hired into their positions have educational backgrounds; however, in recent years, districts have been hiring more superintendents with business backgrounds. Superintendents must also, however, bring expertise beyond an educational background to the position.

In this role, I was accountable for student achievement. A superintendent of any school district needs much more finely honed attributes than tending to the needs of children. Matters related to students accounted for only 30% of my job responsibilities. The other 70% of my priorities and objectives involved skills in which I had no formal background. These new roles posed major challenges for me.

My roles varied. They included marketing the district, negotiating property outcomes, understanding the budget, navigating declining enrollment and population trends, watching over the district's real estate and facility interests, and building relationships with seniors and the Mom-and-Pop businesses of the community. I was tasked with negotiating a variety of disputes, rights of way, and easement issues with the good ole' boys' notorious network of the City Council and City Manager.

I was not technically prepared for these roles. I was not only swimming in new waters, but I required a set of real estate and business technical skills. This included intuiting and navigating power plays with the City fathers, who felt they were the true decision-makers for all aspects of City life. While governance for a school district is within the purview of a school board, Santee City Council members often functioned as if they wielded absolute power, specifically over property, even if the school district owned the property. The property assets of the school district outpaced those of the city. The district paid a retaliatory price in delayed negotiations and zoning for matters over which the city government had decision-making authority.

The City Manager was an egotistical man who represented the interests of the City Council with a vengeance. It occurred to me immediately that my excellent people skills were not enough to meet the objectives of successfully dealing with the City Manager, who was the City Council's representative. When the City Council referred to the district's Governing Board as "the girls," I also recognized that the good ole boys' network on the Council felt that they should be the only entity to wield power over City entities, including over the school district.

Given that the district's property assets were more lucrative than the city's, the district was more powerful in terms of assets. The Council, nonetheless, was determined to challenge the school district's asset power. For a decade, the city blocked the district from selling its land at a fair market-assessed price. While the district's fair market assessment of one of their properties was $12 million, the City consistently devalued that assessment by 50%.

The City Manager presented several scenarios explaining why we could not sell our property. The City used zoning authority to consistently override our interests. As a woman and a new leader, there were many nights when I felt like I could not do the job. The men on the other side of the negotiating table wielded power that was just too firmly established!

## Losing Battles

Faced with opposition from the City Manager and Council, we faced oppositional communication and multiple coordinated efforts to stifle progress. The school district and city met frequently to discuss our property interests, easement negotiations at several schools, safety stop signs, and abatement concerns. Initially, I was friendly during our negotiations. I soon grasped, however, that the City Manager's smugness was a personal barrier to our talks. While he treated me with civility, I could never trust that we agreed on anything. His communication and approaches were condescending. Any agreement reached in a meeting could become a disagreement once I left the table. I often believed the Manager was laughing behind my back at my limited background knowledge of the specific topics we discussed, which were all non-educational. As a result, he continuously circumvented any agreements in any way he could.

After several meetings, two things became clear:

1. The City Manager was ignoring my positional power because I was a female, regardless of the assets of the organization I represented and
2. Because of my limited background in several real estate and property topics, he took full advantage of me and those I served. He was opposed to any outcomes the district wished to pursue.

I was fighting an uphill battle. Negotiations came to a screeching halt, and I had to report back to my Board that we were at a stalemate on many issues. I was embarrassed because, despite my competence, I was unable to represent the school district's interests in these arenas effectively. Many nights, I felt defeated!

Yet, one thing that women possess that many egotistical men do not is the ability to utilize tactics that are not about ego and power but about strategy. Resilient women can be stubborn and relentless, regardless of how many battles they lose. Their grit and determination often help them to prevail. I decided to take a step back and accept that negotiating alone at the table with the City Manager would not yield any kind of agreement. The culture allowed him to wield male authority over my female power.

As much as I hated to relinquish my direct power, I decided to bring our male district business manager to every future meeting with the City Manager and City representatives. I was able to observe the dance and power plays as these men jousted with each other as equals. It was a difficult lesson for me to hand over negotiations to a male figure and a sober concession I made for the greater good of the school district. I trusted our school district's business manager's loyalty and his ability to keep me informed about his discussions with the city. I was able to direct him behind the scenes to counter the City's offers in his direct, equal male-to-male communication with the City Manager. As a result, our business manager was able to resolve issues to our satisfaction. We made slow but real progress on several property matters beneficial to the district and were able to prevail and win a few important battles.

It was a good lesson for me to learn that the *secret sauce* in negotiations sometimes must be in male gender-to-gender communication because males, still in the twenty-first century, believe they are allowed to wield power over females. Male-to-male communication prevailed because the two males —the district business manager and city manager —spoke the same language. I began staying in the background, yet still pulling the strings, giving direction while our business manager was in the forefront and brought us the district wins we needed.

As a woman, you need to know when to lay your cards on the table and when to hold them. Women can be immensely powerful, pulling strings behind the scenes! By playing the male-to-male card cards, we progressed. My Board was happy with the strategies I pursued and the results we achieved.

**Winning the War**

Still, I had another battle to fight. The Board directed me in 2005 to pass a $60 million bond for the school district to modernize its decades-old school buildings so that students in our middle grades could learn in facilities that included science labs. A bond in the Santee community had not received approval for four decades. I understood that this bond, if passed, would present a major miracle to the local and surrounding communities. That said, the battle was an uphill one, one the City Mayor openly opposed and the City Council opposed behind the scenes.

The City Mayor dared to tell me to my face at a public Council meeting that he was not supporting the district bond.

The mayor refused to shake my hand, saying, and I quote: "I am not going to support your bond." Was this gender politics and egregious signs of male power? I think so. I still recoil at that interaction, but this behavior only gave me more ammunition and the resolve to pass the bond.

After a year of meticulous planning and marketing work, despite strong public and private opposition from the "good ole' boys," the district won and passed the bond by a healthy margin of votes in November 2006. Indeed, the community loved the school district. If I may take credit, I was popular in the community, and so were our board members. Remember those *girls* on the Board?

We initially considered removing senior citizens from the ballot to spare them the expense of the bond if it were passed. However, the seniors in the community petitioned to be able to vote on this bond measure and we passed the measure beyond the 55% needed for approval. As I watched the City Manager and Mayor following the passage of the measure, I took silent pride. A woman of color, who had been dismissed more than once by this group of influential male city leaders, had successfully rallied the support of school board members and the broader community. We triumphed because of our political popularity in the city.

**Reflection**

These scenarios occurred more than 18 years ago. Now retired from this position as superintendent, I fully realize that cities and their governing bodies have an overarching purpose that sometimes conflicts with that of other government agencies, such as school districts. That is, to make money for the city by negotiating money-making ventures that support the entire city's interests. However, why did the City leaders fail to advocate for or partner with us? Did gender bias against females blind them to the possibilities that existed for both the city and the school district? Perhaps the City officials feared bond approval might hinder the city's ability to raise city taxes in the future, given that the school district had already increased citizens' tax obligations through the approval of the bond.

If I had been a male superintendent, would a compromise on many matters have been reached? Would both the city and the school district have satisfied mutual interests to benefit the school and city community? Yes, school districts and cities have major competing interests. However, male egos seemed to get in the way of a compromise that could have benefitted both entities!

## LEGENDARY INSIGHTS

Lessons learned as a female superintendent negotiating with city politicians include:

* **Females can overcome political odds in male-dominated environments.** Utilizing skills distinct from those of males and leveraging emotional intelligence can be a winning strategy for success in challenging political environments.
* **Wielding political power behind the scenes can sometimes strategically be more effective for females.** As a female, pulling the strings behind the scenes can be a helpful critical political maneuver to produce results when males feel the need to fuel their egos by claiming power over decision-making publicly.
* **Do not be discouraged by minor setbacks.** Exhibiting patience and perseverance and choosing not to be intimidated by opponents, regardless of the number of battles lost, can eventually lead to significant victories. As my wise mother once said, "There's always a Plan B."

## VOICES OF POWER

Be willing to show up wherever it benefits your students — even if it feels uncomfortable or unwelcoming.

## Chapter II

### LEADING OUT LOUD
### Claiming My Place as Superintendent

*Dr. Marilou Ryder*

My journey to becoming a school superintendent resembled a maze; intricate, daunting, and filled with unexpected twists. For me, it began as a burning aspiration during my years as an educator, fueled by a desire to effect meaningful changes in the lives of students. Yet, I quickly learned that the road to leadership was paved with hurdles, especially as a woman in a male-dominated profession.

I held the title of assistant superintendent, a role that provided a glimpse into the complexities of district leadership. Despite my enthusiasm, I often felt overshadowed by the intimidating nature of the superintendency. What did it really entail? I was aware that superintendents were deemed the "ultimate person in charge," but the specifics of their daily responsibilities remained shrouded in mystery. Each day brought a barrage of state mandates, special interest pressures, and the expectation of relentless accountability.

While I was passionate about shaping the educational landscape, I grappled with the vulnerability that came with the role; the average tenure of a superintendent hovered around a mere 2.5 years. However, the call to lead and influence was too strong to ignore.

I vividly recall the moment I decided to leap into the world of superintendency. After three years as an assistant superintendent, I sought my boss's counsel. "Am I ready for this?" I asked, feeling both excited and apprehensive.

Her response was, "Yes, what's taken you so long?" Her words lit a fire within me. I updated my resume, attended the state's Superintendent's Academy, and immersed myself in literature about the role.

With newfound confidence, I applied for the superintendent position in my district after my superintendent decided to retire. It felt like destiny, but the reality soon struck me hard. The district had hired a search firm to oversee the hiring process, a revelation that left me puzzled. I learned that in-house candidates rarely secured the position when a firm was involved. I felt my heart sink when I discovered I wasn't selected. I had interviewed fairly well, but I lacked the financial background experience deemed critical by the board.

Devastated yet determined, I realized that I needed to enhance my credentials. I enrolled in a School Business Managers Academy, expanding my expertise in district finance. With this newfound knowledge, I extended my job search radius, determined to find a position that aligned with my vision.

My journey was fraught with challenges. I faced several interviews, each time up against a pool of highly qualified candidates, primarily men. During one interview, a search consultant confidently told me I had aced the process and winked, assuring me the job was nearly mine. But when the call came,

I learned the board had chosen a candidate willing to accept a lower salary, a reality check that stung. The politics of hiring were murky, and I often found myself questioning the integrity of the process.

But resilience became my armor. After a year of reflection and planning, my husband and I decided to broaden my search even further. Preparing for the superintendency became an avocation, a relentless pursuit that consumed all of my time and energy.

As I navigated my path toward becoming a superintendent, I recalled a sobering statistic I had once read in a leadership magazine: it takes women an average of seven job interviews to secure a position as a school superintendent. Armed with that knowledge, I approached each opportunity with focus and determination, applying for positions that genuinely piqued my interest.

It was during my sixth or seventh interview that I decided to apply for a job in Fresno County. One Friday afternoon, as I sat at my desk, the recruiter called. He was engaging and shared that it was a great district, but he warned that the pay was on the lower side. He asked about my current salary as an assistant superintendent in Orange County, explaining that the Fresno salary would likely be comparable.

Despite the low pay, I felt compelled to interview and agreed to apply for the position. My husband and I drove five hours to Fresno for what turned out to be a surprisingly brief 40-minute interview, much shorter than my typical hour-long sessions, often filled with performance tests and community evaluations. The seven-member board asked questions in a round-robin fashion, and while I thought I performed well, scoring myself an 8 out of 10, something was unsettling about the shortness of the interview.

When I left, I spotted a couple of familiar faces in the waiting room—two male candidates I had encountered at previous interviews. It was disheartening, but I tried not to dwell on it. Two weeks later, when I hadn't heard anything, I assumed the worst. Then, to my surprise, the recruiter called back with good news: the board wanted to offer me the job. They liked my references and my positive attitude and believed I would be a great fit. However, I had to make a decision quickly.

I asked for a day to think it over. My husband was anxious about the quick timeline, so I called my mentor for advice. "Do you want the job?" she asked. When I expressed concern over the low salary, she encouraged me to negotiate for more once I was in the role. "It's a good district, and you'll do great things there," she said. "These superintendent jobs are difficult to get. Go for it!" With her support, I accepted the position, and the board seemed delighted.

A week later, I met the board members, only to discover that two of them were not in favor of my hiring. Nevertheless, I moved forward based on a 5-2 vote. I was thrilled to be the first female superintendent in the district and excited about applying the knowledge I had gained in my studies and previous experiences to elevate the district to new heights.

As the first year unfolded, I enjoyed my role despite the underlying tensions from internal candidates who had also applied for the position. I launched several initiatives and began working toward implementing a school bond for new construction. However, the nagging issue of my salary lingered.

There was no evaluation process outlined in my contract, so I partnered with the School Boards Association to create one. I presented the evaluation process at a board meeting, where it was approved with the understanding that any potential salary adjustment would depend on performance feedback.

After a successful year, I decided to request a salary increase. I approached the board confidently, sharing my accomplishments and asking them to consider a raise.

"I love being your superintendent," I said, "and I believe I've done some good work this year. I genuinely feel that I deserve a raise, and I'd like you to consider it." However, the response was disappointing.

Everyone blurted out at once, "No way! You're not getting a raise. We don't have that kind of money. You knew what you were getting into when you took this position; you were aware of the salary."

The board president intervened, saying, "Alright, everyone, just calm down. She's just asking us for a raise."

She then shared, "We can't give you a salary increase this year, but we would like you to consider coming back next year, and we will entertain the idea of an increase in your salary. So don't give up hope. We're so happy you're our superintendent."

The following year, we successfully passed the school bond, and I was determined to present a solid case for a salary increase. I spent a month drafting a detailed presentation that included salary comparisons among the top superintendents in Fresno County. I discovered that I was the only female superintendent and, regrettably, the lowest paid despite leading the third-largest district.

I didn't fully grasp the situation until I created the chart, which was something I hadn't considered before. After conducting my research, I made a chart comparing my current salary with a salary range for similar positions. One chart highlighted what I was currently making, while the other displayed where I fell on the salary scale, and it looked promising. I wanted the board to recognize some key themes from my visuals.

### Fresno County School Districts
### 2006-2007 Superintendent Salaries
*Documented in the Public Record 2007*

| District | ADA | Superintendent | Base Salary |
|---|---|---|---|
| Fresno USD | 79,503 | Mr. Superintendent | $205,100 |
| Clovis USD | 36,323 | Mr. Superintendent | $195,000 |
| Selma USD | 6,345 | Mr. Superintendent | $174,682 |
| Sanger USD | 8,600 | Mr. Superintendent | $159,785 |
| Kings Canyon | 9,300 | Mr. Superintendent | $158,626 |
| Sierra USD | 2.300 | Mr. Superintendent | $141,007 |
| Kerman USD | 3,708 | Mr. Superintendent | $131,640 |
| Coalinga-Huron | 4,073 | Mr. Superintendent | $130,503 |
| West Fresno | 990 | Mr. Superintendent | $130,000 |
| Central USD | 13,500 | Marilou Ryder | $127,477 |

## Fresno County School Districts
## 2006-2007 Top Ranking ADA Districts
### *Documented in the Public Record 2007*

| District | ADA | Superintendent | Base Salary |
| --- | --- | --- | --- |
| Fresno USD | 79,503 | Mr. Superintendent | $205,100 |
| Clovis USD | 36,323 | Mr. Superintendent | $195,000 |
| Central USD | 13,500 | Marilou Ryder | $127,477 |
| Kings Canyon | 9,300 | Mr. Superintendent | $158,626 |
| Sanger USD | 8,600 | Mr. Superintendent | $159,785 |
| Selma USD | 6,345 | Mr. Superintendent | $174,682 |

Additionally, I knew I needed to present a specific number, so I reached out to my state organization for advice. I asked them, "What do you think I should aim for in terms of a salary increase?" I mentioned that I was currently making $127,477 and wanted their input on a reasonable figure for my raise.

One of the male consultants suggested I aim for $135,000, while another male salary expert cautioned me not to go over $140,000. I felt compelled to push a little higher, considering I would still be one of the lowest-paid superintendents in Fresno County and the only female leading one of the top ten districts. If I proposed $140,000, six male superintendents in smaller districts would likely be making much more than I was. That didn't seem right.

The consultant noticed my agitation and pushed back, advising, "If you go in asking for anything more than $140,000, you'll embarrass yourself. Trust me, aim for around $135,000. That would be over an 8% raise, something your board could accommodate. I know these Fresno people."

I've always relied heavily on my husband's advice, especially regarding issues that arise from working in a male-dominated work environment, so I turned to him for his recommendations. I shared the consultant's suggestion, and to my shock, he exclaimed, "Are you crazy? You need to go in at $160,000!" My heart raced as I thought, "Oh my God, what do you mean—$160,000?"

I reminded him that one consultant had warned me not to ask for more than $140,000 or I'd risk embarrassing myself. My husband replied, "If you ask for anything less than $160,000, I'll be the one embarrassed for you." I cringed, feeling a wave of anxiety wash over me. He had seen the charts and knew what the other superintendents were making. I had always trusted this man, and at that moment, I made my decision: I would go in asking for $160,000 armed with my charts, graphs, and positive evaluation.

The board consisted of four women and three men, with three of the women being prominent figures from the agricultural community; their husbands were also farmers. What I learned about working in Fresno is that these women, who owned and managed farms, were incredibly empowered and fiercely independent. As they looked at the chart, I noticed two of them becoming visibly upset, more than I had ever seen in a board meeting.

"Look at this chart! She's the only woman here," one of them exclaimed, her voice rising. Another chimed in, "Yes, and she's the lowest paid! We didn't know this!"

The tension in the room thickened as the board president turned to me and asked, "Dr. Ryder, what salary increase would you like us to consider?" My heart raced, and I could feel the weight of their gazes on me. I took a deep breath, looked her straight in the eye, and said, "I'd like my compensation to be $160,000."

They nodded, but I could sense the mixed emotions in the room. "We're going to meet and discuss this. Go home, and we'll call you later tonight with the results," they said.

As I drove home, my nerves were on edge. I didn't feel like I had embarrassed myself. Nobody reacted too dramatically to the $160,000 request; they all simply nodded. But the three men in the room didn't look too pleased, and that uncertainty loomed over me like an all-too-familiar Fresno storm cloud as I awaited their decision.

About an hour later, after a glass of wine and some anxious moments, the board president called. She said that the board wanted to clarify if my $160,000 request included a cost-of-living adjustment (COLA)—a salary increase designed to keep up with inflation and rising living expenses.

I replied, "No, it didn't." She paused for a moment and then said, "Okay, we'll call you right back." As I hung up, I thought, wow, that was interesting.

About half an hour later, the phone rang. "Dr. Ryder, we'd like to raise your salary to $162,740. We're very proud of you." My heart raced as I processed their words, and then they added, "We'll put a memo out to the press tonight." I was flabbergasted. She didn't mention anything about me being the only female; the only thing she said was that I deserved the raise.

The following morning, I picked up the Fresno Bee from my driveway—and the moment I flipped it open, I gasped. On the front page, it boldly announced that the superintendent received a salary increase of $35,263, with a quote from the board president stating, "This hefty increase brings the district—the third largest in Fresno County—more in line with what other top schools in the county are paying their leaders." The article also included quotes from people in the district, including the teachers' union president, who said, "Well, good for her. She deserves it."

The very next day, I attended a monthly meeting with all the county superintendents. As I walked in, I was met with an unexpected wave of recognition. The deputy county superintendent stood up and declared, "If anyone wants to know how to negotiate a raise, you need to talk to Marilou Ryder!"

To my astonishment, all the men in the room began clapping. At that moment, I felt a surge of pride and validation. While this was a personal victory, it also served as a testament to the progress we were making for women in leadership. I realized that my journey was not only about securing a fair salary but also about inspiring others to advocate for themselves.

As the applause continued, I realized I was no longer just a voice in the crowd; I had stepped out from beyond the shadows and was ready to pave the way for more women to follow in my footsteps.

## LEGENDARY INSIGHTS

Here are some top tips for women educational leaders preparing to negotiate their salary with a board of education:

* **Do Your Research:** Gather data on salary ranges for similar positions in your area, including the average pay for superintendents and administrators. Utilize resources like salary surveys, district reports, and state education associations.
* **Know Your Worth:** Compile a list of your accomplishments, contributions, and any unique skills that set you apart. Highlight specific initiatives you've led and the positive impact they've had on students and the community.
* **Prepare a Solid Case:** Create a presentation that clearly outlines your achievements, the rationale for your desired salary, and how it aligns with the district's goals. Use charts and data to support your argument.
* **Practice Your Pitch:** Rehearse your negotiation conversation with a trusted mentor or colleague. Focus on confident body language, clear articulation of your points, and responses to potential counterarguments.
* **Stay Professional and Positive**: Approach the negotiation with a collaborative mindset. Express gratitude for the opportunity and emphasize your commitment to the district's success.
* **Be Open to Feedback:** Listen to the board's perspective and be willing to discuss their concerns. Flexibility can

lead to a more favorable outcome, even if it doesn't meet your initial request.

* **Own Your Worth:** Women often hesitate to ask for what they're truly worth, while men tend to negotiate more confidently and aim higher without hesitation. My husband reminded me of this. He said, "Why not ask for more? You've earned it." That moment stuck with me—it was a reminder that, as women, we often undervalue ourselves even when we've more than proven our capabilities. Leadership is also about knowing your worth and not being afraid to claim it.

# VOICES OF POWER

Building a culture rooted in intentional connection to our 'Why' is the path to excellence.

# Chapter III

## THE DAYS ARE LONG, BUT THE YEARS ARE SHORT

*By Cindy Petersen*

As a mother of four amazing children and seven grandchildren, the phrase "the days are long but the years are short" has long resonated within my heart, reminding me of how fleeting life and these moments are. Were it only possible to hold on and savor deeply these moments before, in the blink of an eye, it seems, they are gone.

This is also how I felt as I stepped into retirement in 2023 (and still do today as I write this). It did not seem remotely possible that twenty incredible years had passed in my role as superintendent of Gateway Community Charters; yet, inevitably, the time had come, and retirement was at hand.

As I considered this opportunity to share a message with women leaders, this idea of how quickly time passes rose to the top, along with a sense of urgency. We only have so many days - so many years- and the fact that they pass so quickly creates a sense of urgency for us to support, celebrate, recognize, and empower current and emerging women leaders.

I've identified four practical areas that have empowered me and I believe, have also empowered other women leaders (with a little creativity in their titles). Hopefully, these will resonate with you as well.

***"Nobody puts baby in the corner."*** *"Dirty Dancing" finale*

I will never forget the advice a fellow woman leader gave me on this topic. I had been part of a series of meetings where, due to the nature of my role and knowledge, I should have been leading the conversation and its outcomes. Yet, as I expressed to this friendly ear, I was frustrated and felt "sidelined." Her advice to me was a huge "a-ha" moment, revealing that I, in fact, was responsible for the sidelining. How could this be? Without realizing it, I had ceded both the head of the table and the leadership of the meetings by showing up at the same time and choosing to sit on the sidelines, I had signaled exactly where I saw myself.

So, for the next meeting, I showed up a little earlier and — as you may have guessed — I sat at the head of the table. By my mere physical presence, I had previously given away my voice, and with this new action and presence, I was able to step into the leadership that was, in fact, already mine.

So where are you sidelining yourself? What will it take to get you to the table and off the sidelines? Remember, you do it for yourself, and you do it as a model for others. When you take your place at the table — when you find your voice and speak up — you create the space and the permission, if you will, for other women to do the same.

***"The truth will set you free."*** *John 8:32*

Author and management expert Ken Blanchard (2001)[4] credits his colleague Rick Tate with the saying, "Feedback is the breakfast of champions." Unfortunately, the research suggests that women often receive less and less helpful feedback than their male counterparts. Feedback that is timely, well-intentioned and direct is a gift. Feedback should be given frequently and often and, as often as not, as a positive affirmation of what the individual is doing well.

Throughout my career, I've had few opportunities to receive direct feedback that truly supported my growth. I remember at one point being called into the assistant superintendent's office with no real understanding of the purpose of the meeting, only to be told, "You're too intense" and "You don't have a sense of humor" without any context at all. I didn't report to her directly, and it wasn't part of any formal evaluation—yet to this day, I still don't know what it was all about. (Although, to her credit, I own my passion and intensity.)

So, how might we do a better job of giving feedback? First, we must check our hearts and be sure we have a clear and appropriate intention to help the other person. Once our intent is clear and we have made it known to the other person, we can then provide direct, clear, and caring feedback. We dialogue with the other person about what we see, hear, and understand — providing examples as needed, answering questions and concerns, and committing to follow up and offer coaching, resources, and additional feedback as necessary. And for the faint of heart, whose sense of concern and compassion rises up at the thought of giving feedback, author and researcher Brené Brown (2018)[5] reminds us that "Clear is kind."

And what about receiving feedback? If we're honest, few of

us get excited about the opportunity to receive feedback, and for this, Brené Brown further suggests the mantra, "I'm brave enough to listen." If we desire to improve and grow, and we stay brave enough to listen and self-reflect, feedback truly propels us on our leadership journey.

*"Go ahead and jump!" Van Halen*

Sheryl Sandburg and others have noted the research on gender differences and career advancement. First and foremost, we must recognize that there are cultural and systemic issues that create an uneven playing field, with men still earning, on average, more in salary than women and also being offered more advancement opportunities. Studies also suggest that men may be better at self-promotion than women.

So, what can we do? First, as women, knowledge is power. You, too, need to learn the fine art of self-promotion. As women, we need to understand our worth, recognize what we bring, and find ways to ensure our organizations acknowledge and value our contributions. Second, as leaders (male or female), we need to mentor, coach, support and guide our women leaders in building their confidence and owning their accomplishments. Lastly, once we have done those things, as leaders and peers we can help them find the opportunities to "go ahead and jump" with confidence into new roles and opportunities in their career pathway. And if you're reading this as a woman leader, take this as your sign to go ahead and jump!

*"Celebrate good times, come on!" Kool & the Gang*

When we find ways to recognize and celebrate the

accomplishments of women leaders, we lift them up, and we provide models for emerging women leaders. Over the last 20 years of my career, I watched the Association of California School Administrators (ACSA) and others grow in this endeavor. ACSA birthed and nurtured the Women's Leadership Network, encouraging regional and state-level activities that brought together women leaders. Other entities also grew in their efforts. The California Association of Business Officials (CASBO) now holds an annual Women in Leadership Conference. Many colleges and universities now offer women in leadership certificate programs.

During my time in leadership, we created and nurtured a women's event that started by honoring a local woman leader and grew over nearly a decade to celebrate and recognize women leaders across multiple regions. For many years this event was a highlight for the regions involved, with approximately 300 women coming together to celebrate women leaders. Unfortunately, the pandemic took its toll on the event, but each of the regions is now finding its own way to honor women leaders — and so the legacy continues.

So, what can you do? Don't wait for ACSA or similar organizations in your state— affirm, celebrate and recognize women leaders in small and not-so-small ways at the team level, the school level, the district level, and the county level. It's up to all of us!

As a retired woman leader, I remind you — the days are long, but the years are short. Before you know it, like me, you'll be retiring from this wonderful calling of educational leadership.

Your time is now, and you need to focus with intention on what you can do to support and empower yourself and other women leaders on the leadership journey. We're counting on you! And for my fellow women educational leaders out there ... I leave the "arena" and our children in good hands — you've got this.

## LEGENDARY INSIGHTS

* **Take your place at the table – Stop sidelining yourself.** When you show up with confidence and claim your space, you not only lead by example but empower other women to do the same.
* **Feedback is a gift – Embrace feedback as an opportunity for growth.** Remember giving and receiving clear, direct feedback helps everyone thrive and improves leadership effectiveness. Be brave!
* **Know your worth and promote it – As women, we must recognize our value and confidently advocate for ourselves.** Consistent and appropriate self-promotion is key to career advancement, and mentorship can help build the confidence to "jump" into new opportunities.
* **Celebrate the success of women leaders – Recognizing and honoring the accomplishments of women creates a ripple effect of empowerment.** Whether big or small, celebrations uplift leaders and inspire others to follow suit. Each of us – lifting up all of us!
* **Time is fleeting, so act with intention.** The years pass quickly, and as women leaders, it's crucial to seize every opportunity to support, empower, and celebrate others, leaving a lasting legacy for future generations. Your time is today – live it, love it, grow with it, and celebrate it... for yourselves, your peers, your sisters, your daughters and those to follow.

A leader's greatest power is knowing when to stand tall and when to stand back.

# Chapter IV

## FIRST WOMAN EVER

*Dr. Carol Riley*

Story of my life. First woman ever to be on a swim team. Always boys. First woman ever to try out for a football team. Always boys. And then:

*First Woman Ever* was the headline in our small-town weekly paper—marking my selection as the first woman principal of an elementary school and the first woman ever to hold a principalship in the district.

Growing up, the only career options available to women were typically limited to secretary, nurse, or teacher. So, I decided I would become an executive secretary. I attended college, but the classes were boring. I could already type really fast. I could take shorthand unbelievably well. I could talk to people. So, I looked at my college roommate. She was having lots of fun. She was going to be a teacher. So, I switched majors.

When I took Music for the Elementary Teacher, our professor announced that the final exam would require us to get up in front of the class and teach a song. She reassured us, saying, "Don't worry, most people can carry a tune, even if they think they can't."

Fast forward to my turn. I stood up, ready to teach my song, and started. Moments later, she stopped me mid-song.

Turning to the class, she said, "Remember when I said very few people can't carry a tune? Well, you" (pointing at me) "are one of them. Stop. And promise me this: if you ever become a teacher, never sing to children!" *Ouch.*

Anyway, I became a second-grade teacher, and true to my word, I didn't sing to the children. After that, I taught fifth grade, then moved on to middle school as a special education teacher. My last teaching assignment was at the high school level.

However, I eventually grew bored again. I wanted something different, a new challenge. I was still young and eager for a fresh experience. (To this day, though, I've stuck to my promise; I still don't sing out loud!)

I decided to pursue a career in school administration. I loved schools and teaching, but I was ready for something new. So, I set my sights on becoming a principal. Every principal I'd ever known was a man, but I knew I could do the job just as well, if not better.

I applied. Twelve people were interviewed for the job. I was the only woman. After all the interviews, I was called and told I was the successful candidate. Once I took the job, people shared that I was the only woman in administration and that I would likely face challenges. But they believed in me. I believed in them.

I was successful. I became a principal and served in that role for four years. Later, I moved to a larger district and was appointed principal again. At that time, a few other women were serving as elementary school principals, but men still held all the principal positions in the middle and high schools.

After three years, I moved to another district in a different county. Following my interview, the superintendent offered me the position and asked if I preferred to be an elementary principal or a middle school principal. He mentioned there were no female middle school principals in the district.

I thought about it carefully and decided that taking on the middle school role would be a good step forward in my professional growth.

I loved the new challenge. The sixth, seventh, and eighth-grade students were wonderful. The teachers had a different energy than the elementary teams I had known for so long, but the fit was right for me. I genuinely enjoyed my new role in the district. The superintendent was engaging and approachable, someone who built strong relationships with both teachers and administrators. He became my hero—someone I admired deeply. Watching the way he led with connection and respect, I found myself thinking that my next step would be to become an assistant superintendent.

Before I knew it, an assistant superintendent position was posted in my district. I was confident in my work, and I knew my superintendent appreciated it. All the higher-level positions in the district were held by men. I didn't care. I submitted my application anyway. Sure enough, I got the job.

At one point, I was meeting with other high-level administrators, and they asked me why I didn't speak up more in the meetings. I told them that sometimes, the best thing for me to do was to listen. Then, when I did talk, others would listen to what I had to say.

The assistant superintendency was fun and fulfilling. I still wanted more and decided to apply for the top leadership role in education, the superintendency. I applied for a position in a smaller district in a different county and successfully secured the role. Once again, I was the only woman among the applicants. At that time, there weren't many female superintendents in California. I was one of the lucky ones to get the job.

I truly loved my role as superintendent, but after a few years, I decided I wanted to take on the challenge of leading a larger district. I found a district that seemed like a great fit and applied. I ended up being the district's second choice, and this time, I did not get the job. Despite my confidence, things didn't work out as I had hoped. My husband and I had almost purchased a house in the district, but it just wasn't meant to be.

After losing out on another superintendency opportunity, my husband was offered a position in Hawaii. We both agreed it was an excellent opportunity, so he moved ahead while I stayed to complete my superintendency contract. Once it expired, I retired and joined him in Hawaii.

Shortly after moving, I discovered that the Head of Schools for Hongwanji Mission School was searching for a leader to run their school. I applied for the position and they offered it to me. They didn't care whether I was a man or a woman; they valued the breadth of my experiences. It was yet another exciting new chapter in my career.

This was a private Buddhist school, and the majority of students were Japanese. Along with gaining new educational experiences, I had the opportunity to learn about and immerse myself in a new culture.

In retrospect, I look upon my career with admiration. I've loved every job I've taken on and succeeded in all of them. The success did not come from being a man or a woman. It came from a higher source. It came from the ability to walk in humility, to be grateful for the blessings in my life, and to worship my God with gratitude.

Still, I smile, knowing that in more than one district, I carried the headline: *First Woman Ever.* And I walked through that door, knowing it would never close behind me.

## LEGENDARY INSIGHTS

* **Embrace New Challenges Fearlessly:** Success often comes from stepping into uncharted territory. Whether it's being the only woman on a swim team, applying for roles traditionally held by men, or taking on leadership in a new cultural setting, bravery in pursuing opportunities can lead to incredible growth and fulfillment.
* **Listen to Lead:** True leadership isn't about speaking the loudest; it's about knowing when to listen. By observing and understanding others, you can make impactful contributions that carry weight and inspire respect.
* **Believe in Your Unique Value:** Gender doesn't define capability. Confidence in your skills, experiences, and ability to adapt can open doors, even in male-dominated spaces. Know your worth and let your work speak for itself.
* **Find Gratitude and Humility in Success:** Achievements are built not only on hard work but also on a foundation of gratitude and humility. Recognizing the blessings in your life and remaining grounded can lead to sustained success and meaningful leadership.

# VOICES *OF* POWER

Always take your lunch break.

## Chapter V

# LEADING THROUGH THE STORM

## Building Trust When Civility Breaks Down

*Dr. Patricia Clark White*

Once upon a time, in a very conservative corner of Southern California, a school district shocked the community by appointing a young woman as its new superintendent, a bold move that few saw coming. As a former assistant superintendent of what was then called personnel, my current superintendent urged me to apply for this top position. I did not expect that I, a woman, would be selected. After just four years as an assistant, I wasn't sure I was ready for all the dynamics involved in the top job.

As assistant superintendent, I dealt with strikes, walkouts, and grievances, none of which could be described as civil. However, I now had the responsibility of establishing a trusting relationship with a new school board, new union leadership, new faculty, and the new community.

One of my first challenges in the role was handling a board member whom the others openly described as a bully. He lacked civility, steamrolling others to get his own way. The other board members felt terrorized and manipulated by him, often allowing him to push through decisions they didn't support, all out of fear. To build trust with the board, I had to demonstrate that

I could get this bully under control. However, I also wanted to maintain a working relationship with the bully board member, if possible.

I learned an important lesson about bullies from an early experience in my life. As a first grader, I had to walk home from school by myself every day in snowy neighborhoods. Three "big kids" (probably second graders) followed me home, pushed me down, and put snow down my back. When I reached home crying to my mama, she told me that bullies understood only one thing: You must stand up to them.

She said the next time they came after me, I was to turn around, put my hands on my hips, and tell them, 'No!' I did as she suggested the next day, and, to my amazement, it worked! However, what I didn't realize at the time was that my mother was standing behind a tree and stepped out in full view of the bullies while my back was turned to her. Lesson learned: You must stand up to bullies, or they will continue to steamroll right over you. However, it's good to have backup!

When facing my first board conflict, I applied this lesson by speaking individually with each board member about the importance of standing up to bullies and the value of sticking together and supporting one another during critical confrontations. The bully board member's strength came from his willingness to depart from civility. The remaining board members' strength came from a desire to stand together firmly and civilly. They agreed to adopt this principle and were able to change the bully's behavior in a remarkably short period of time. I also learned the importance of helping board members develop skills for this unique role by coaching them with respect and support. The civility and unity they demonstrated with him helped us all maintain a positive and trusting working relationship moving forward.

Labor negotiations often put superintendents in situations rife with incivility. When it becomes clear that the parties may not reach their goals, angry community members frequently pack board meetings. Union leaders often view the superintendent as the primary obstacle to achieving their goals.

As a new administrator, I recall sitting in board meetings and observing how superintendents approach these situations in two distinct ways. The first way was to argue with speakers about the veracity of their claims. Sometimes, I would see a lack of civility coming from the superintendent as well as the podium speakers. In my judgment, this did not go well. It exacerbated the situation, making it much more difficult for the parties to regain trust afterward.

The second type of situation I observed was a superintendent who maintained a quiet and positive demeanor, listening with respect to each speaker, and at the end, commenting to the board president that he would carefully consider all the points made that night, keeping in mind that the board was required to cut $8 million from its budget in order to stay solvent and avoid a state takeover. In situations where civility has plunged to new depths, it's easy to want to give back as much as you get! However, that does not usually provide the most productive outcome.

I have had my share of board meetings with speakers at the podium castigating me for failing to fund salary demands.

Using the lessons I learned from watching other superintendents handle these very complex, emotionally charged, and frankly somewhat hurtful exchanges, I decided to use the approach of the second superintendent.

Engaging in a shouting match in public does not earn public respect, especially if you hold a position of power. It causes your opponents (and onlookers) to have less esteem for you and enhances their drive for vengeance. I also felt that it was essential to keep the big picture in mind, which was that these disagreements would eventually come to an end, and rebuilding trust would be crucial for the district's well-being. The death of civility can also lead to the death of trust. Taking the High Road may be the only thing that can keep trust on life support during these dark times.

One of the toughest moments I faced as a superintendent was standing before the board and recommending the closure of a school. It wasn't just a professional decision, it was personal. Schools aren't just buildings; they're communities, memories, and a source of stability for so many families. Knowing that my recommendation would affect teachers, students, and parents made it one of the most difficult decisions I've ever had to make.

We were facing a budget crisis that involved millions of dollars in cuts, and we were reviewing everything. Early in the school year, I had a very frank conversation with the board about a school that had fewer than 200 students and an overhead that included a full-time principal, a full-time secretary, a 6-hour clerk, support personnel, custodial services, as well as energy costs, supplies, and other expenses.

I acknowledged to the board that there may be other solutions than closing this school. Therefore, I suggested that we establish a district-wide committee with representatives from each school in the district to consider the issue and provide recommendations. We provided this committee with information and support. After several months of meetings and reviewing various options, the committee recommended closing the small school. I provided their report to the board, and we had an open session to discuss it.

The board unanimously accepted the committee's report to close the school, but a packed house on the night of the board meeting raised the stakes. Many speakers and signs held by others reflected a lack of civility and untrue statements. While the board was somewhat prepared for the decision, I hadn't realized that one of the board members attended the same church as several parents from the neighborhood school. After Sunday services, they approached her and had a very emotional conversation about it. She agreed to support them in looking for other options.

This was a blind spot that I had not anticipated—the personal connection between community members and board members. She persuaded the board to request that the committee reconsider its options and explore alternatives proposed by community members from the school that was slated for closure. This sudden change led to a rift between the committee and the board, which rejected their recommendation. Also, a rift existed between the school community members who felt abandoned and the district. Board members were upset with each other for breaking apart at the last minute. So how do we fix all these problems?

It was crucial for me, as superintendent, to demonstrate compassion for those whose school might potentially close, as well as respect for the work done by the committee. I had to coach board members to adopt similar outlooks, looking past current concerns and toward a positive outcome. I began by meeting with the school community at their school and listening to their concerns and alternative solutions.

They had a representative on the committee, and I asked her to bring a written list of their proposed alternative solutions to a committee meeting. The Board President and I met with the committee to express our sincere appreciation for their tireless efforts over the past several months. We also expressed our commitment by carefully considering every alternative. We committed to transparency, honesty, and fair dealing with the process. We showed our support by attending every meeting until the issue was resolved, and we invited the target school to send three representatives to observe.

The committee reviewed every alternative proposed by the school community and analyzed the potential impact of each one. Ultimately, they reaffirmed their original recommendation and presented the board with a detailed analysis of all considered alternatives, along with a clear rationale for their final decision. Although the neighborhood school community remained unhappy, they felt they had been given a fair hearing and were willing to accept the outcome. The board accepted the committee's recommendation, which helped resolve the tension both between the committee and the board and among the board members themselves.

What is the biggest lesson I took away from this experience? Always give every alternative a fair hearing, be transparent about how decisions are made, and approach even the most challenging conversations with compassion, especially when you're facing people who may seem like adversaries.

After being verbally attacked in public at both the board meeting and on TV, it's not always easy to maintain a kind and civil approach with your attackers. However, it is crucial to build trust for a working relationship to continue. Smart leadership also demands us to consider potential blind spots in the political relationships that may exist among decision-makers and their constituents. I had failed to do that, and it caused a rift in board relationships and committee trust. Fortunately, the other steps taken to resolve the situation helped us regain trust in our relationships.

Trust is the bedrock for successful leadership, and for a superintendent, it's everything. Without trust, nothing else works. My position did not entitle me to trust. I had to earn it every single day. Trust requires a great deal of hard work. It does not happen by accident. Without it, I would have no followers and I would be unable to deliver the vision for my organization without them. Without trust, I would not have the support of my board of trustees, and without that, I would not have survived as a superintendent for very long. Without trust, the very survival of my organization would be at risk. It required honesty, transparency, respect, and keeping commitments.

Since the death of civility can endanger trust, it was critical to zero in on that dimension as well. Compassion, grace, patience, and tact had to become a way of life. Some may dismiss sensitivity and thoughtfulness as too feminine for the top job, but these traits are essential for preserving civility and building trust.

Trust and civility aren't just nice to have; they're essential for the long-term survival of any organization or career. After 21 years as a superintendent, I felt blessed to work with incredible colleagues and mentors who taught me the true power of these two elements. Learning how to build trust and lead with civility has become a guiding force in both my leadership and my life.

## LEGENDARY INSIGHTS

Although I spent 21 years as a superintendent for three different districts, I never stopped learning important lessons about being a successful leader. Here are some of the ultimate lessons that shaped my career.

* **Trust is the bedrock of good leadership.** If people don't trust you, they are not likely to follow you. A leader without followers cannot deliver the vision needed for the organization to survive. Building trust with board members, stakeholders, partners, and associates is essential to good leadership. This requires honesty, transparency, and keeping commitments.
* **Taking the high road can keep trust on life support during dark times.** When people are hurling metaphorical rocks at you, it's hard not to lob a few back. However, it's more important to focus on the long game rather than short-term satisfaction. When disputes are resolved, trust must be rebuilt. This will be easier to do if the leader maintains civility even in the face of unfounded accusations.
* **Every alternative must be given a fair and transparent hearing.** Sometimes, a solution seems so obvious that it is easy to expedite a decision. However, those with a stake in the outcome may have other creative ideas. It has been said that "people are more interested in getting their say than in getting their way." Frequently, those in an adversarial position usually want assurance that

decision-makers have truly considered their input. Once they believe others have fairly analyzed their suggestions, they become more willing to accept the final decision.

* **Sensitivity and thoughtfulness go a long way toward maintaining civility and trust.** While these are typically considered feminine traits, they are valuable assets in building trust. Compassion for those who may be negatively affected can help us to react with grace, patience, and tact. This type of civility helps to build trust and long-term relationships.

# LEGACY TRUTHS

Success isn't about fitting in — it's about standing out with purpose.

## Chapter VI

## THE UNLIKELY CANDIDATE

*Dr. Linda Kimble*

One very late night, during a school board meeting, an all-male panel abruptly terminated my boss's contract—and, much to my shock, turned to me and placed me in his seat. At thirty-eight, I was a single mother of two young children, unexpectedly entrusted with leading their school district. I hadn't asked for the role, nor had I interviewed for it. In fact, I'd been the district's assistant superintendent for less than six months.

The board had a tumultuous relationship with their prior leader, and apparently, I represented the exact opposite. The departing superintendent was an older, more reserved male, and I was a young, enthusiastic female. "Why did you choose me?" I asked the Board President.

"I saw leadership and energy in you," was his response. He recognized my potential long before I did. This was the first of many times I found myself the unlikely candidate.

I've learned that the best way to understand something is to dive in and get involved. I approached the cluttered office of my predecessor as if I were on a treasure hunt. I began calling the names listed on the letterhead of the many letters stacked on his desk. Each call was a window into an issue he had been handling, and I would simply begin by asking, "Can you tell me about this situation?"

Much to my dismay, I quickly discovered that many district issues had been left unresolved, such as bond measures, construction concerns, and a lack of funding for several already-approved projects. For example, the district had failed to pass a school construction bond before bringing high school students back through the unification process. As a result, there was no funding to build the facilities needed to house them.

What a tremendous hurdle for a new superintendent! I didn't have a coach or mentor to guide me; I just had a willingness to give it the old college try. And so, I did. I rolled up my sleeves and jumped in. That's how I learned my first real lessons as a superintendent and developed the knowledge of school funding and construction that I still carry with me today.

There were significant challenges in this tiny, rural district. As superintendent, I had the bus dispatch radio on my desk. I was asked to participate in everything from climbing on leaky roofs to driving roads to determine if schools would be closed due to flooding. I loved the adventure of these tasks and approached them with both enthusiasm and a keen interest in learning.

Attending leadership events reinforced my sense that I was an unlikely candidate for leadership roles. The lack of women in the room at superintendent conferences was striking—only about 13% of all superintendents in California were female at the time. And those who were present were typically twenty years my senior. As a newcomer to the role, I often felt like an impostor. But I was fortunate. A few seasoned female leaders took me under their wing. They were knowledgeable, warm, and generous with their support—helping me find my footing when I needed it most.

I never felt shut out or dismissed by my superintendent colleagues, regardless of their gender. In fact, I remain deeply grateful to them for their support and kindness. They helped me resolve major facility issues in my small district and provided sound guidance during some of my most challenging moments. Their example stayed with me, and I made it a personal commitment to do the same for the women leaders who would come after me.

One of the lessons I learned is that once you are a superintendent, you will always be considered "superintendent material" until something goes terribly wrong. (And things can easily go wrong!) However, that tiny district provided me with the experience and credibility to move forward. I will always be grateful to the board president and the confidence of this small district.

**Sound of Music**

After gaining my footing and earning the respect of my colleagues, I stepped into a new chapter—this time as superintendent of Anaheim, a much larger and more complex district. Once again, I was viewed by some as *the unlikely candidate*. But by now, I was familiar with that role—and ready for the challenge. In Anaheim, the city is famous for its most popular theme park, but oddly, the elementary schools lacked musical instruments. Decades earlier, music education had been eliminated due to budget cuts, and locals still remembered the day the instruments were sent back to the music stores, like Willy Wonka shutting the doors to his chocolate factory.

A local nonprofit adult orchestra composed of professional musicians was eager to see our students develop the skills needed to one day join their orchestra. Sharing a deep belief in the power of the arts, the orchestra's leader and I resolved to find a way to bring music back to our schools. Neither of us had the money or support to make it happen, but we were united by a shared conviction that the future opportunities for our students made the fight worthwhile.

We began connecting students to orchestra members who volunteered to offer after-school instruction. Then, we reached out to local neighbors and friends, asking them to check their closets and attics for unused instruments. The local chiropractor donated a cello. Soon, the instruments began trickling in, then pouring in to support the program. Of course, there were critics, both on the school board and within the district. What did this superintendent and this orchestra leader know about funding and running a comprehensive district-wide music program? This was a good question. But we learned as we went, driven by determination. Where there's a will, there's a way.

As time passed, the School Board supported the hiring of music teachers. School and district-wide music programs were born. The program grew and then exploded with enthusiastic learners. North American Music Merchants (NAMM) started featuring the program, co-designing it with us, and promoting it broadly across the United States. Disney, Yamaha and many others provided supportive funding.

Fast forward to the future: In 2022, 2023, and 2024, Anaheim Elementary School District was named the Best

Community for Music Education by the NAMM Foundation. Were we the most likely candidates to build a music program in the *Happiest Place on Earth*? Probably not, but we were courageous and energetic enough to give it a try. Where there's a will, there's a way.

**If You Build It**

As the daughter of a builder, I've always believed in the lasting impact of school buildings on both current students and future generations. In my first rural district, I discovered that only one building on the high school campus had been appropriately approved by the State Architect. Our practices of housing students in non-approved buildings frightened me. Even more alarming, the gymnasium had been constructed with materials that were not permitted for school use, making it impossible to approve. Yet, despite this, the gymnasium was used every single day.

Again, as the unlikely candidate, I started learning about the Division of State Architect, which materials were and were not approvable, and how buildings might be redesigned. I met with designers and builders, visited the State Architect in Sacramento, and researched methods for providing housing for our students.

Later in my career, building a performing arts center and other structures with the team provided me with tools to help schools grow and construct for the future. All-male construction meetings were the norm. I found myself walking on construction sites in a skirt, hard hat and the tennis shoes you brought for the occasion, again wondering if I seemed like the unlikely candidate.

In Anaheim, there was a significant need for school facilities. Working with the board, we put a bond on the ballot. The bond passed, and schools were funded. What a great feeling it is to see student housing move from concept to reality! The same happened in the next district, where the passing of a bond became my first focus. Would I have guessed I would end up focusing on school funding for construction? Never.

Today, as a former superintendent, one of my chosen roles is helping school districts fund school bonds to build schools for the future. It's a fitting continuation of my journey as the unlikely candidate, someone who often stepped into roles I never anticipated, driven by a commitment to making a difference. I am grateful for the opportunity to help others create an enduring legacy, ensuring safe, inspiring spaces for generations of students to come.

## LEGENDARY INSIGHTS

* **Rethink the Résumé:** The unlikely candidate may be a great fit. They bring a different perspective. Have confidence in your candidacy.
* **See What They See:** Sometimes, others will see leadership in you that you do not see in yourself. When someone points to you as a leader, believe them.
* **Lead with Spark:** A little enthusiasm goes a long way. Energetic leadership is contagious. Sometimes, it is not the tallest, fastest or smartest person that gets the lead role; it is the most enthusiastic.
* **Willpower Wins:** Where there is a will, there is a way. Trust your leadership and confidence to set challenging goals and do what is best for students.

# VOICES OF POWER

We're all messy and imperfect — no more or less than anyone else. Own it, grow, and keep moving forward.

## Chapter VII

## GRACE UNDER FIRE

### A Superintendent's Story

*Dr. Marylou Wilson*

Not many people are aware of this, but between March 2020 and September 2022, ninety-four female superintendents left their positions in the nation's 500 largest school districts. Some stepped down voluntarily, while others retired; however, many were quietly pushed out. Sixty-six percent of them were replaced by men (ILO Group)[6]. The reasons varied, yet a troubling pattern emerged: women who had led through one of the most challenging periods in modern education, navigating school closures, public health crises, and political turmoil, found themselves burned out, scrutinized, and, in many cases, forced to step aside. The very leaders who had held school districts together in the darkest of times were suddenly no longer welcome.

This is my story, a tale of one superintendent who refused to back down in a time of crisis and chaos, proving that women not only survive in leadership but excel.

Growing up in a large family, I never realized that being a woman would make a difference in the workplace. In our home, which often had six children and extra teenagers at any given time, everyone pitched in, and hard work was expected.

At fourteen, I started working, first under the table, then legally once I had my driver's license. I took on minimum-wage jobs throughout high school, quickly learning that I didn't want to do any of those jobs for the rest of my life. College became my goal, and once I saw it as attainable, I never looked back.

I chose teaching because I honestly felt like I could do it better than most of the teachers I had growing up. I remember sitting in class thinking, 'There's got to be a better way to explain this,' or 'If they just approached it differently, we'd all get it.'

From the beginning, I felt confident in my ability to manage a classroom and deliver effective instruction. Yet, that confidence wasn't always welcomed. Early on, I was advised to keep my opinions to myself and learn from the more experienced teachers, most of whom were women. But I wasn't one to sit back and wait. I earned a master's degree, found joy in the daily adventure of teaching, and soon set my sights on a career in administration. The pace, the problem-solving, and the ability to impact an entire school energized me.

When I left a tenured teaching position to become an assistant principal, I was warned by a woman, no less, that I was taking a dangerous risk. I could lose my job, and then what would I do? However, I wasn't one to stay safe at the expense of growth.

As an assistant principal, I enjoyed the daily challenges, never knowing what each day would bring. Moving forward, I climbed the leadership ranks, taking on a variety of roles in different school districts. Each step, though daunting, fueled my passion for leading at a higher level. I had seen too many ineffective leaders, and I believed I could do better.

Eventually, I became a superintendent in a district where privilege and poverty coexisted. The district was financially stable, but it had suffered from turmoil, board recalls, high superintendent turnover, low morale, and a lack of trust between employees and leadership. Stepping into that environment was no easy feat. Community members were deeply involved, serving on committees and attending district events. Slowly, I worked to rebuild relationships, restore faith in leadership, and guide the district forward.

And then, I faced the biggest challenge of my career. It was late Friday afternoon, March 13, 2020. My Emergency Team stood in my office, urging me to close schools indefinitely due to COVID-19. I hesitated. Public schools are the backbone of our country; they provide structure and safety for families and shutting them down felt like pulling that foundation out from under our community. But as the hours passed and surrounding districts announced closures, I had no choice. I agreed to shut down for two weeks, believing it would be a temporary measure. Then, the governor issued a statewide lockdown.

Overnight, my role changed. I became an expert in viral transmission, vaccines, masks, and hospitalization rates. I was in my office daily, navigating a crisis no one had prepared me for. I hadn't signed up for this, yet the burning sense of responsibility for students and families kept me pushing forward.

Every challenge I had faced, breaking into administration, proving my leadership in districts fraught with distrust, and stepping up in the midst of a global crisis, had prepared me for this moment. I realized that leadership isn't always about certainty; sometimes, it's about stepping forward when no one else wants to. And so, I did.

Initially, the focus across the nation and in our school district was at a very basic level. We were making sure our families had access to food, shelter, and medical information. Although we were closed and students and employees were home beginning March 16, 2020, I showed up to work that day and every day after. I knew I had to be there to make sure everything that needed to be done actually got done.

Once we were declared an "essential business," I was able to bring in Food Services Staff and Maintenance Staff. We began distributing meals daily, and then, when the rules became more reasonable and flexible, we were able to provide weekly meal kits to the families. I was there every day with our food services team as they prepared meals for any family in the area. It was incredible to see our staff pouring their time and energy into supporting the community. The all-female food services team came together not by design but by chance and we were determined to make sure every student was taken care of and fed.

The maintenance team also worked with me daily, ensuring that the buildings stayed in good condition and that the "essential construction" projects had the oversight they needed. I later realized that if I was there, they were there. If I stayed late, they stayed late. They were an incredible team of men who respected my leadership and had my back every step of the way. They looked out for me and made sure I was always safe and I'm truly grateful for what they did for me.

Once basic needs were met, I was able to focus more on the educational needs of our students and what we owed them as a public institution. During that first month, my executive cabinet was working from home and in April, I asked them to start coming to the office one day a week. Setting up meetings with them was a challenge. Brainstorming, creating, dreaming and trying to figure out what we could do over Zoom felt overwhelming. I wanted them in the room with me. At first, they came in on separate days, and although that worked for a while, they eventually realized how valuable it was to be in the workplace together. They asked if they could come to work with me every day, and of course, I said yes!

My executive assistant, otherwise known as my right arm, was with me as much as possible. As a mother of two, she managed Zoom school at home and supported a superintendent and governing board. Life for everyone became very complicated very fast.

One of the long-standing structures in our district that I used for managing wildfires, floods, air quality, and other emergencies was what we called The Emergency Team. The group was comprised of leaders from all aspects of the District, including Governance, Educational Services, Union Leadership, Parent Groups, and Maintenance. Initially, as we were in the throes of the pandemic, The Emergency Team met frequently to maintain open lines of communication and provide updates across the departments. This team was critical, and each leader was required to stretch their learning and become an expert in COVID-19 within their area of expertise. The information gathered and shared in these meetings was disseminated to the public through Parent Forums and during a standing item at Governing Board meetings, as appropriate.

From the day I agreed to close the physical classrooms and have the students learn from home, my goal was to get them back into our buildings. In the meantime, union leadership and administration reached many agreements and found common ground, which created schedules for students to attend instruction at home via Zoom. Public education is a highly relational process and young people do not learn well virtually. Having witnessed Zoom classes where students were rolling around on the floor, in their pajamas, or sitting on their mothers' laps, I knew this situation was not ideal or sustainable.

One of the factors that supported my leadership during this challenging time was the leadership in the County Public Health Department and the surrounding school districts in the county. All the leaders in these positions were women and all of us were proponents of in-person instruction. The public health doctor met with us weekly at first, and then biweekly once the crisis had calmed. She, too, wanted children in school, not at home.

We spent a great deal of time with her talking about the science and the medical aspects of COVID-19, and we stayed away from any of the politics. She educated me in a manner that allowed me to educate my Board, employees, students, and the school community. I was able to be clear, concise, consistent, and honest about what I knew at that given moment. I remember using some of the phrases she suggested like: "We are doing the best we can with the knowledge we have today", and "If we had experienced COVID-19 before, we would have been better at knowing what to do next."

In our community, the state's COVID-19 Outbreak Color Chart prevented us from reopening for in-person learning at the start of the 2020–21 school year in August. It was deflating; I was sure we were ready. The Emergency Team, now known as The Transition Team, had taken every measure to ensure the safety and security of students and staff. We had plans for everything.

The Governance Team, comprising my Executive Assistant, one School Board Member, and me, prepared back-to-school presentations for the Board, employees, and the community. The Wellness Committee ensured that each site had an isolation area, a testing area, thermometers, and other essential supplies. Food services were ready to continue grab-and-go breakfast and lunch daily. The Facility Team relocated desks, installed desk shields, added directional stickers, upgraded air filters, and performed additional tasks.

The Instruction Team worked with teachers to focus on core academic principles, knowing the shorter day meant letting go of some content. The Technology Team ensured students and staff had the necessary tools for both in-person and remote learning. Teachers adapted to providing live instruction through cameras for students at home, and some students needed hotspots to access their teachers' Zoom rooms.

We were ready, just waiting for the chart to finally turn in our favor and it did. In-person instruction was set to begin in

October, and it felt like we were finally turning a corner. But then, on September 29, 2020, everything changed. Again.

The Glass Fire was a devastating wildfire that erupted in Northern California's Napa and Sonoma counties. Fueled by dry conditions and strong winds, it quickly spread, burning for over 20 days and consuming more than 67,000 acres of land. The fire destroyed over 1,500 structures, including homes, wineries, and businesses, and forced tens of thousands of residents to evacuate. Families, wineries, and businesses lost everything. COVID-19 was at the bottom of the list at this point; people were in hotels, shelters, friends' homes, or anywhere they could find safety. My school community was in crisis and once again needed the feeling of safety and having food and shelter mode.

After six years as the district superintendent, guiding the school community through several tough crises, I could feel their trust. They believed in me; they knew I'd lead them through this one too. Since starting in July 2014, we have faced a major earthquake, an armed robbery, severe flooding, previous fires, COVID-19, and now this new major fire. A primary focus since 2014 has been safety and security, ensuring a warm, safe, and dry environment. We had emergency plans, schools had practiced, and students knew what to do in the event of an emergency. The Glass Fire broke out over the weekend, and evacuations began early in the morning, disrupting virtual learning. It was chaos. Teachers, students, and classified staff were unable to log into Zoom. There was no electricity, no internet, and, for some, no homes. Families were evacuated once, twice, and sometimes even a third time.

For the first time during the pandemic, I was unable to go to work as the roads were closed and the town was completely evacuated. I called on the Transition/Emergency Team to meet with me if they were able. The top priority of the meeting was simple: Are you OK? Is everyone OK? Each leader was tasked with checking in with their employees and compiling a list of who had lost their home, where they were, and where they would be in the short term. The reality was that, at this point, no one was willing to discuss anything other than the fire. Balancing the need to care for people with the work that still needed to be done was a challenge. I'm not sure I always found that balance, but I'm sure if you asked some of those who worked in the district, they would say I failed.

As the fire began to diminish, I was back on track and ready to move forward with getting everyone back to in-person education. The first challenge was convincing the executive cabinet that it was the right move. I remember telling them, "If I'm wrong, you can go to the rooftop and scream, "I told you so!"" I just knew in my heart, my bones, and my being that children needed to be in school and teachers needed to be with them in person. And I was willing to do anything necessary to make this happen. Fortunately, we had the resources to make it happen and we did. The Director of Maintenance later told me, "Dr. Wilson, I did not even know what you were asking me to do, and I researched it and did it, and it worked and kids are here and safe. I am so grateful because my daughter is one of them. What we are doing here is amazing."

The Transition Team continued to work its magic and did everything possible to ensure the safety of our students and employees. We met with the Governing Board and presented a plan that included a delayed start date of one week, putting us into the first week of November 2020. We had to allow the fire stress to settle. We had to clean up the ash from the fire. We had to ensure the schools were clean, safe, and welcoming. Or at least as welcoming as possible, with everyone wearing masks, walking in designated patterns, staying in small groups, and having their temperature taken every time they entered the classroom.

We were told that to open for in-person education, we had to provide COVID-19 testing sites for all employees at one of our sites. The administrator assigned to this task resisted, uncertain about the safety of returning to in-person learning. When I realized the hesitation, I met with the school nurse and became her teammate on the project. We had to make it happen and open school. And it was a simple task that became a luxury for our employees. Many found it helpful and gave them peace of mind as they chose to be tested on a weekly basis. We trained staff members to run the testing center, and I was there to visit with them, thank them, and talk with the employees who chose to be tested.

We opened the first week of November 2020 and it was truly a glorious day. Approximately 75% of our students came to in-person instruction five days a week for five hours a day. I began visiting every school every week. I went into the classrooms, shared my appreciation with the teachers, and said hello to the children. The first time I saw student work on a classroom wall, I took a picture and sent it to the Governing Board.

Some of the employees were not happy with the decision to return to in-person education and had no trouble letting me know. I listened to them and kindly disagreed with them. I was resolved in my belief that students and teachers needed to be in classrooms together working and learning in person.

After being in school for about a month, we approached Winter Break. The Executive Cabinet suggested that, due to the holiday, we might consider moving to virtual school for a couple of weeks following the holiday to minimize the risk of COVID-19 spread from family travel. I was frustrated and disappointed. Why? If we added virtual learning, families would travel longer. I knew our community. Some would travel if we would let them. And remember, we had families in poverty, and they needed the school system to allow parents to work.

I held my ground; we came back to in-person instruction immediately following the Winter Break. In addition, after surveying teachers, I learned that the live virtual instruction was not working for many students. We were required to offer it to families in need, and we continued to do so. After January 2021, parents were required to prove that need. By March 2021, 95% of our students were attending school in person in our district.

During January, vaccines became available for COVID-19. One afternoon, late in the day, I received a call from the hospital asking if I could arrange for 20 employees to visit the vaccine center. We were informed that once a vaccine had been opened, it had to be used. It was a joy to be able to call employees and share the news that they could visit the vaccine center and receive their first dose.

Unfortunately, most of the employees had left for the day, so I was unable to fill in the number they had asked for. However, I decided I would go and receive my first dose. Within the next two weeks all employees in our district were vaccinated with their first dose of the COVID-19 vaccination. Soon after, our facilities became vaccination sites for the entire community.

Fortunately, the last few months of the school year continued with little controversy. State testing was cancelled. There were no field trips scheduled. Parents were overwhelmed with the cancelation of prom, mass graduation, field days, and more. Our high school principal was brilliant and developed a plan that was approved by County Public Health to allow each high school senior to graduate individually with their family. Additionally, he and his vice principal visited every home to post a graduate sign on the front porch of the senior's home. This became the most impactful moment of his career, as it opened his eyes to the reality that many of his families lived in actual poverty, yet they were still happy and healthy.

The 2020-2021 school year ended with a COVID-19 infection rate of less than 3% in our schools. Students and employees followed the instructions we provided to ensure their safety, but some individuals still contracted the virus. Most people did not. We were fortunate. We put numerous safeguards in place, and they worked. I asked everyone to work harder than they had ever worked in their careers, and they did. I told them it would be difficult, and it was.

My career plan was to retire in 2020 or 2021. I could not do it. I was amidst a crisis, and I was compelled to see it through to the end. I had been with the district since 2014, and I knew that new leadership would be a challenge. Superintendents were leaving districts in large numbers, and many were working from home, not opening their schools. I wanted to see it through. I told my husband that once I got the schools open, I would retire. I successfully opened up all the schools, but I knew I couldn't leave yet. I needed to give it one more year.

I finally announced my retirement from full-time work for June of 2022. In hindsight, if I had to do it over, I think I would have stayed longer. When I reflect on it now, I realize how fortunate I was to have stayed the course. Many female superintendents didn't get that chance. In just over two years, nearly 100 female superintendents from the nation's largest school districts left their positions, some by choice, others not. The majority of them were replaced by men. The very women who had held school districts together in the darkest of times were suddenly no longer leading. But I stayed. I led through the storm. And I left knowing that I gave it everything I had.

Recently, I had a conversation with my former executive assistant. She told me that she and some colleagues now understand that, although they may not have always known why I wanted them to do something, they now realize it was always centered on integrity, honesty, and putting students first.

In a field where women are often underestimated and pushed aside, I proved to myself and others that leading with values, especially in turbulent times, truly matters. Even when the storm raged, I stayed true to my purpose. I led through the storm and I hope my journey helps other women realize they can too.

## LEGENDARY INSIGHTS

The lessons I learned from being a female superintendent stem from a quote that guided me throughout my entire leadership journey, as shared by Garrison Keillor (1995)[7]: "Nothing you do for children is ever wasted."

* **Trust what your gut is telling you.** Even when others tell you something else, trust your own judgment and what you believe is right for students. Listen to the facts and the science, and do what you can to quiet the noise of the media and politics. If you can do so, you will make the best decisions to move forward. It is not always easy, and sometimes you may be wrong. And this is where you must be willing to admit a failure and move forward.

* **Be willing to show up every day and in every way.** Even when it is challenging, and potentially even dangerous, you must remain visible and available to your entire community, especially during times of crisis. They need to know how much you care and that you are willing to go the extra mile before they will listen to how much you know.

* **Build capacity in your staff and allow them to soar.** As a superintendent you cannot be an expert in everything. You can, however, be an expert in building capacity in others. You must establish a structure within your organization that ensures employees receive the necessary training and professional development to perform the tasks required for their positions today and in the future. They need to know they are valued and important and

that they are expected to take the lead within their layer of the organization.
* **Build a culture where risk-taking is celebrated and honored.** If risks are not taken, you will always get what you have always had. You must create a culture where your employees not only take risks but thrive on innovation, creativity, and venturing into the unknown. During the COVID-19 crisis, we were unsure what to expect when we returned to school in person for five days a week, and as it turned out, it was successful! Just think how much our students would have missed in their education had we not taken that risk.

*Side note: During the annual business audit the following year, we received a 'finding' for not posting the Williams Act Hearing as required prior to the Governing Board meeting.* When I questioned the auditor and mentioned that to do so, my Executive Assistant would have had to break through road closure barricades and National Guard presence in order to post, he mentioned he understood. He still made it clear it was a 'finding' with no remedy. Could you imagine? My talented assistant running through fire to post a ridiculous piece of paper notifying the public that we will hold a hearing for the Williams Act. I honestly found this one to be ridiculous. In all this mess, she was evacuated but managed to post the notice on the district's website.

# VOICES OF POWER

Mentor with purpose: Lift as you climb – the next generation is watching.

# Chapter VIII

## The Day the Dead Guy Drove to School

*Dr. Lillian Maldonado French*

### The Emergency

What do you do when a shooting victim crashes his car into an elementary school parking lot? The school principal called me immediately after the incident, her voice rushed and clipped, offering only the barest details before she ran outside. A two-car shootout had erupted just down the street from Nelson Elementary right at dismissal time. One of the vehicles had crashed into the school parking lot. My mind raced to the students and families who might have been walking home and caught in the chaos. Then the principal reminded me that Open House was scheduled for that evening, meaning students would be released early. The street and lot were, by sheer luck, empty. Relief mixed with urgency. I turned to my secretary. "Call the board members, tell them there's an emergency." This was before smartphones, before instant notifications. Then I grabbed my keys and jumped in my car to help.

The events of the past year rolled through my head as I raced to the school, one of four schools in the Los Nietos School District, a K-8 district in unincorporated Whittier. The day had begun normally enough; we were in the middle of our Open House season, with each school scheduled on a different night.

As a first-year superintendent, my focus that week was on visiting schools and spending time with our district's families. Two years prior, I began my career in Los Nietos as the Director of Education, which in a small district meant I was responsible for all aspects of teaching and learning. My position provided me with regular contact with teachers and aides but limited contact with non-instructional classified staff.

In the spring of the previous year, our superintendent announced his retirement and asked each of his three directors if they were interested in the job. I decided not to apply, remembering how challenging the relationship among school board members had been in my previous district. I loved curriculum and instruction, and the small size of Los Nietos ensured I had a hands-on connection to the classroom. The thought of having to work with Board members was not terribly appealing. I also assumed that, as the newest director and the only woman, I was unlikely to get the job. That summer, I agreed to serve as interim superintendent while the Board made its selection.

I threw myself into the job, planning for the new school year and learning to work with the Board. I quickly learned that I loved the superintendency. While building relationships with five very different personalities was challenging, I found that I truly enjoyed hearing their points of view and working to develop a cohesive team. I invested the time to create a strong communication structure and to establish governance protocols and Board goals. Since no one replaced me as the head of instruction, I continued to do that work as well. The difference was that now I was setting the direction for the entire district, aligning Board goals with instruction, operations, and human resources. Within two months, the Board inquired about my interest in the job, much to the disappointment of another director. So, just like that, I was appointed the first female superintendent of the district instead of the male district administrators. The news caught the school community by surprise.

I spent considerable energy during my first year as superintendent dealing with the politics of being appointed. Although the teachers knew me and were generally receptive, the teachers' association was upset that they were not given the opportunity to participate in the process. The classified staff was even less pleased, and since many lived within the district boundaries, they had a greater influence on the community. Parents had expressed concerns about the safety of the schools and the neighborhoods in general. While the Board expressed confidence in my work, my position in the district felt tenuous.

## The Glass Cliff

The American Association of School Administrators (2025)[8] reports that while women make up approximately 75% of the teacher national workforce, they account for only about 28% of all superintendents. Of the 28%, only about 10% represent women of color. In California, the number of women superintendents is higher, but it still falls short of being representative of the population. For example, based on 2019–2020 data from the California Department of Education[9], Latino students represent approximately 55% of the student population.

That school year, there were 371 women superintendents and approximately 47 Latina superintendents. Therefore, women represent 37% of all California superintendents; however, Latina superintendents make up less than 5%. The numbers are even smaller for Black and Asian or Pacific Islander women superintendents, and the disparities do not end there.

Robinson, Shakeshaft, Grogan, and Newcomb (2017) examined hiring differences among superintendents based on gender and race. They found women superintendents were more likely to be hired from within the district than from outside. Female superintendents were likely to have been elementary principals with a background in curriculum and instruction, while male superintendents were more likely to have been high school administrators. Women superintendent career paths often include extended stays in staff-level positions rather than the more direct pipeline experienced by males (Sanchez-Hucles & Davis, 2010)[10]. The data also suggest women superintendents of color face additional barriers.

Instead of the traditional "glass ceiling," researchers have introduced the concept of the "glass cliff" to describe the career trajectories of women of color (Chiefs for Change, 2019; Sanchez-Hucles & Davis, 2010)[11]. This term reflects the heightened risks these women often face when placed in leadership roles, which are frequently high-stakes and precarious. The consequences of failure in such roles tend to be more severe, further compounding the challenges they encounter (Chiefs for Change, 2019, p. 9)[12]. This phenomenon also occurs in the superintendency. Arriaga, Stanley, and Lindsey (2020)[13] found that school boards often place women superintendents of color in urban school districts with high percentages of English learners, low-income students, and students considered at risk. Their research shows that school boards frequently expect these women to turn around struggling districts while offering them very little room for error.

These statistics line up entirely with my career path, making me feel a bit of a cliché. I worked only in low socio-economic, high English learner school districts. In each of my career advancements, I waited until someone tapped me on the shoulder and suggested I should apply. I became a superintendent almost by accident, and then I had to contend with the political fallout. Given the political reality of my position, this emergency was a high-stakes situation and I found myself on a glass cliff.

**The Crime Scene**

Five minutes later, as I pulled up to the school, I saw a crowd of residents and staff in the school parking lot. Emergency vehicles had just arrived, and the police were trying to control the crowd. The principal informed me that the vehicle had gone under the chain link, like a giant squeegee curtain at a car wash. The car then hit and ricocheted off several parked cars before finally crashing into a low block wall. Most teachers were on campus putting the finishing touches on their classrooms before the Open House, but thankfully, no one was in the parking lot at the time. The kindergarten classrooms were closest to the parking lot, so those teachers were the first to reach the vehicle. They found the driver unresponsive, with a bullet wound to the chest. The principal reiterated that the area was empty due to the early release day, and no one on the street or in the parking lot was injured. The emergency personnel quickly took over and soon left with the injured man to the hospital.

At this point, the police took over and began their investigation, processing the crime scene and taking statements from the witnesses. I stood in the parking lot with the police as they received word that the suspect had died on his way to the hospital. This had just become a murder investigation. I quickly made my way through the school gates and stood on the sidewalk.

Police detectives arrived on the scene and immediately secured the campus, preventing anyone from entering or leaving until they had processed the crime scene. They gathered the staff in the library and converted a classroom into an interview room.

## The Communication Problem

I stood outside the campus just hours before Open House, with the school still on lockdown and teachers and staff inside. Meanwhile, concerned residents gathered at the gates, questioning whether it was safe to send their children to school. Additionally, most parents still thought there would be an open house and would arrive on campus within three hours. Canceling Open House with nothing more than a notice on the locked gates would send the wrong message. At that time, the district did not have a robocall system or other methods of mass communication. I rushed back to the District Office to devise a plan. First, we needed to hold some type of Open House for a school on lockdown for the evening. It was important to communicate that our schools were safe places for students and to reassure them that we were meeting their needs.

After sending a team to drop off pizza for everyone under lockdown at the school, I contacted the superintendent of the Whittier Union High School District, where our students attend once they leave us. Pioneer High School was two blocks away from Nelson Elementary School, so I asked if we could redirect families to their multipurpose room and hold a meeting there. Next, I asked if we could use their robo-call system to contact the school families and inform them of the meeting. The superintendent readily agreed to help, and I had our district's lone tech person reach out to their technology department. Their techs solved the problem by creating a phantom school on their student data system. Our tech person drove over to the student information (this was the time of CD-ROMs) and uploaded the data. Then I recorded a message for families, informing them about the meeting at the high school that evening and the rescheduling of Open House. I sent the message, checked in with a few parents to ensure they received it, and breathed a sigh of relief; I had 90 minutes before meeting with the families. Suddenly, shivers went down my spine, my stomach turned, and I had a visceral flashback to one of the worst experiences of my administrative career.

As a first-year principal, I had the honor of opening a school. I hired all the staff, and together, we spent days developing a vision and building a foundation for the future. We evolved into a tightly knit community. So, it was beyond devastating when toward the end of our first year, authorities credibility accused one of the school's most beloved teachers of inappropriately touching a student.

I had received all the necessary training on protocols for handling initial information, contacting the proper authorities, and supporting students and families throughout the police investigation. My district contacts were the Assistant Superintendent of Personnel and the Director of Elementary Education. I also felt confident in my communication skills and my ability to guide the school through the crisis.

I sent a letter to families informing them of the situation, held regular staff meetings to provide updates, and met individually with those who needed to discuss the matter further. To keep the staff united, I continually reminded them that our priority was the students.

It was not our job to determine guilt or innocence; it was up to the police to decide whether to charge the individual. I dealt with the media circus outside of the school's gates each day as best I could. I also tried to create a sense of normalcy and a focus on learning.

By the second week there was a feeling that we had arrived at a quiet, if uneasy, normal. The cameras were gone, the campus subdued, yet parents still had questions. I had a sense that I needed to bring our families together and provide them with the same support that I had been giving the staff. My district office contacts didn't think this would be effective, but I forged ahead, thinking that I knew my community best. A few evenings later, I had a packed auditorium of parents looking expectantly at me and my district contacts, who were there to offer support.

After a brief update on what could be shared, the three of us stood at the front of the room, ready to answer questions. What ensued was every administrator's nightmare. One parent stood up and demanded to know explicit details of the case. When I replied this wasn't possible, parents began to yell that I was covering up to protect the teacher. Then another parent screamed that we had no proof and we should stop our scapegoating. Other parents yelled questions and demanded to know what we were doing to keep their children safe. I continually tried to bring order to the meeting, but I had lost control. People were screaming at each other, some standing and pushing against one another.

I looked over to the district administrators for help only to see them quietly making their way to the door. They left me alone to face what was turning into a mob. I heard comments such as "That woman doesn't know what she's doing." At one point, the parent of the child who had made the accusation stood on a folding chair and yelled that his daughter was lying and nothing had happened. I wanted to cry.

I honestly don't remember how the meeting ended, but gradually, as the audience finished venting, people began to leave. I realized I had made a rookie mistake. Rather than make space for good communication, I had given bad actors an opportunity to spread rumors. Luckily for me, this was before the advent of social media. That experience stayed with me, strengthening my resolve never to let it happen again.

## The "Open House" Meeting

I called the high school principal and asked her not to set up chairs in the multipurpose room. Then, I put together a list of talking points outlining the facts of the event and our plans to ensure student safety. I contacted the school board members, inviting them to join me and the other district administrators that evening. I asked the principal to invite any interested staff members who weren't in lockdown and to instruct everyone to arrive half an hour early.

Once a dozen of us had gathered in the empty multipurpose room, I distributed the talking points and positioned the school board members and administrators in a receiving line near the entrance. Rather than waiting for the meeting to start, I stood near the door and greeted people as they entered the room. I informed them that, instead of a formal meeting, they would have the opportunity to speak directly to the Board. I then introduced them to the Board President standing to my left, and he shared one or two talking points. After a brief conversation, he handed the individual to the board member to his left. The goal of the conversations was to reassure families that we were working with the authorities to ensure student safety.

Once the family member had met with the Board, a district administrator or a school staff member would come over to engage with them. They eventually thanked them for coming and informed them we would be rescheduling Open House in the near future. We continued this process for a couple of hours until the last person had left the multipurpose room. Because people arrived at different times, there was never much of a wait to speak with the Board. Community members exited the room feeling heard and with a better understanding of what had occurred. The board members were extremely pleased with the opportunity to speak with their constituents and listen to their concerns. It was a very different outcome from my greatest nightmare.

## The Aftermath

After the meeting I went back to the school to see what was happening there. The staff had finally been allowed to leave, and only the principal, the school custodian, and the district maintenance team remained. The maintenance team had repaired the fence and all were waiting for a tow truck to arrive to take the vehicle to an impound yard as evidence. I convinced the principal and school custodian to go home while the maintenance team and I stood waiting until close to midnight. Despite being asked repeatedly, I wouldn't leave until we all left together.

I spent the time telling stories about my family, my father's work in construction, and learning about their families. The next day, I heard from the head of maintenance that his team had been impressed with my willingness to stay with them. I noticed a difference in the way I was greeted by non-instructional staff when I visited schools. Many made an effort to come up to me and say hello. Word had spread among the classified staff, and I had earned their respect.

These two incidents highlight the crucial role of effective communication in crisis situations. While frequent and clear communication is essential, choosing the correct method is just as important. Having personal conversations with the Nelson community, rather than a group meeting, gave families an opportunity to share their concerns and feel heard. Today, we have numerous choices for instant digital communication, but sometimes, only a face-to-face conversation can convey the care and concern that each side expresses. Another insight is the need to give board members opportunities to enhance their communication skills. The adage of having one spokesperson on the board is correct, but all board members benefit from learning how to communicate effectively during a crisis. Providing them with training in crisis communication is a worthwhile investment.

Another learning takeaway is that people watch what you do, not what you say. For the three years in the district, I had worked hard to develop good relationships with the classified staff. While seen as someone friendly, they weren't willing to trust me until they saw me stand beside them in an emergency. Although it was a small gesture, we fed the teaching staff during lockdown, and they appreciated it. Both associations noted that I worked hard to meet their needs during a difficult time. The goodwill I gained from this experience was invaluable as we faced financial challenges during the Great Recession.

Ultimately, these incidents highlight the value of creating opportunities for mentoring. Having a mentor when I was a principal may not have avoided the meeting from hell, but it would have been wonderful to have had their support. No matter your current position, someone is coming up behind you who can benefit from your experience and guidance. While glass cliffs may not always be avoidable, a mentor who listens and shares their experiences can make all the difference.

## LEGENDARY INSIGHTS

* **Intentional Communication**: Carefully consider which type of communication best fits each situation based on the issue, goal, and audience. The quickest type of communication may not be the most effective. Plan out in-person conversations and take the time to actively listen, rather than just imparting information.
* **Building Communication Capacity:** Provide opportunities for members of your school community to improve their communication skills. Give opportunities to learn and practice crisis communication before it is needed. As a superintendent, it's especially important to offer this support to Board members.
* **Modeling with Integrity**: People learn from what you do, not what you say. Be aware of the messages you are sending through your actions and body language. Be impeccable in your word and deed.
* **Mentorship and Networks**: Make opportunities for mentoring. Reach out to those in lower positions and offer your support. Find experienced and successful administrators in the positions you are interested in and ask for their advice. Establish a system of support among your peers.

The best leaders build benches, not pedestals.

# Chapter IX

## WHIPLASH TERRITORY

*Dr. Myrna Rivera Coté*

For thirteen years, I navigated the turbulent, high-stakes world of school district leadership, serving as superintendent in four vastly different communities. Although all are located within the same large county, their demographics, student populations, and political landscapes vary dramatically. What they shared, however, was an unwavering commitment to their children's education, a passion that fueled both inspiration and intense debate.

Each district's Board of Education was a unique blend of individuals with differing levels of educational expertise and political aspirations. Some were deeply invested in student success, while others seemed more concerned with power plays and personal agendas. In three of the four districts, I held the distinction and the burden of being the first woman appointed as superintendent. It was both an honor and a test, a breakthrough moment wrapped in unspoken expectations, scrutiny, and the ever-present challenge of proving I belonged at the head of the table.

My previous position as deputy superintendent of a large school district, combined with the knowledge gained in my doctoral work, provided me with the skills and confidence to lead the education side of a K-12 school district. However, especially for my first superintendency, I knew I would need to supplement my business skill set by relying upon the expertise and leadership of the Assistant Superintendent of Business in each district. Unfortunately, the competency of the individuals in this position varied significantly and did not always measure up to my needs and expectations.

Stepping into my first superintendency was anything but typical. I wasn't just leading one district; I was navigating the complexities of two distinct school districts, a K-8 and a 9-12 secondary district that functioned as a single, unified system. It was a rare and challenging structure administered by one superintendent and governed by one Board of Education. The previous superintendent had previously held the position of Assistant Superintendent of Business and was highly regarded by the Board. Given the Board members' opinion of my predecessor, I naively assumed that the business side of the district was functioning efficiently. I therefore focused my efforts on the numerous educational challenges I encountered.

This superintendency tested me at every turn. The Teachers' Union wanted to be superintendent; the Board wanted to be superintendent. I was hired to be superintendent, and it was my first superintendency. I had so much to learn and no time to ease into the position. To succeed, I depended on my dissertation chair, a former highly respected superintendent to mentor me through many challenging issues that had never occurred in my previous district or in the doctoral case studies I had reviewed. The daily highs and lows of this roller coaster ride were extreme.

I often refer to this superintendency as my "whiplash" position due to the many times I said, "You did what?!?" during staff meetings. A perfect example of this was when the Director of Education Services asked me if, this year, the district *could* follow the State's Textbook Adoption Guidelines. It appeared that these guidelines had been consistently disregarded. The practice followed was that high school teachers decided what textbooks they wanted to purchase, and to maintain peace with the Teachers' Union, the district proceeded accordingly. New textbook adoptions for the K-8 schools had been ignored for years.

After surviving my first year as Superintendent, I dared to hope that the worst of the challenges were behind me! The education side of the district was running smoothly, and sound leadership and guidance were provided by the newly empowered assistant superintendent and her staff. The schools were improving academically with targeted professional development opportunities and accountability measures. I was better informed and closely monitored the district's personnel issues and quirks.

As the first woman superintendent, I was met with a warm welcome, and I enjoyed my increasing involvement in the city's traditional customs and activities. By contrast, the Teachers' Union was very difficult and antagonistic throughout my tenure. Their leadership had routinely beat the previous superintendent into submission with behaviors I was not about to tolerate. In addition, the Board members continued to question the numerous changes I needed to make to bring the district into regulatory compliance and focus. I explained each issue using as much data as possible to eliminate the perception that I was making changes for the sake of change. I pushed the Board to focus on thoughtful improvements that added real value and elevated our processes for the benefit of our students.

One day in late July, as I began my second year, a routine visit to the district office prompted me to start questioning whether the business side of the district was truly running as it should. The Director of Technology approached me. He was excited and eagerly shared that he had just been informed by the Assistant Superintendent of Business that he had two weeks to spend thousands of dollars on technology for the schools. He indicated that getting this type of information at a late date was not unusual. I explained my concern that late notification of grant funding meant that there was no time for him to spend the funds adequately and responsibly. He literally had no time to assess what was needed districtwide.

I was very curious about the source of this sudden financial windfall and why it was being distributed so late. According to state regulations, the district's budget was presented to and approved by the Board in a timely manner. Appropriations were set for all schools and departments for the upcoming school year. However, as we prepared to open the second school year of my tenure, I suspected that I was about to open Pandora's Box and experience one of the worst "whiplashes" of my career.

After confiding in a few trusted mentors, I reached out to a highly respected consulting agency and hired them to conduct an extensive financial analysis of the district. I was frank with the Board as to the need for this extra expenditure. There was strong pushback because everything "had always been fine with the previous superintendent". However, after clearly and directly expressing my suspicions, I received the support I needed. I had worked with the leadership of this consulting agency in my previous district, so they rearranged their calendar to help me immediately.

Despite relentless roadblocks and withheld documents, the consultants pressed forward, determined to uncover the whole financial picture. The Assistant Superintendent of Business resisted their requests at every step, and I often had to intervene. The consultants' persistence and constant updates helped prepare me for the unsettling findings I would eventually have to share with the Board of Education.

As mentioned earlier, this district operated as a unified system, encompassing both elementary and high school levels. Annually, each division received separate financial allocations, grants, and supplemental funding. Due to the higher costs associated with secondary education, the high school district consistently received a larger amount of funding than the elementary district. High schools traditionally spend more money than elementary schools, in part due to course requirements, additional personnel, and after-school sports, among other factors. This meant that each budget should have been monitored closely to ensure compliance with Board of Education priorities, as well as secondary and elementary state and federal mandates.

The consultant's final report revealed a critical issue: instead of carefully monitoring expenditures throughout the fiscal year, the business department had a practice of balancing the district's budget by backfilling secondary shortfalls with unspent funds from various sources, including elementary district surpluses, unused grant funding, and other leftover allocations. In addition, what became glaringly apparent was that my first year's annual budget had been balanced without needing to use the technology grant funding, making the grant ultimately available to be given to the Director of Technology to be spent as initially designated. There were many other findings in the final financial report, but this one was the most unnerving. My suspicions regarding the "sudden" allocation of grant funds to purchase technology were legitimate.

The Board of Education was stunned by this revelation. Their reactions ranged from shock and frustration to deep concern. Without hesitation, they issued a series of directives outlining immediate personnel and procedural changes that I was to implement. One Board member was deeply affected by the findings. His tenure as a Board member was long, and he was a good friend of the previous superintendent. He came to see me soon after the findings became public and apologized to me for not paying closer attention to the budget. He also apologized for bringing me into this situation. I appreciated his apology very much.

Unfortunately, he chose not to run for reelection to the Board, a loss that I felt significantly. His support would have been invaluable to me as I continued navigating the relentless white-water rapids throughout the remaining four years of my tenure as superintendent in that district.

That first superintendency tested me in ways I never could have imagined, stretching my leadership skills, patience, health, and resolve to the limit. But it also made me stronger. I learned to expect the unexpected, stand firm in my moral and ethical convictions, and keep a steady hand on the wheel because, in Whiplash Territory, the only way to survive is to stay balanced, adapt quickly, and never lose sight of the destination.

### LEGENDARY INSIGHTS

* **Attend annual fiscal and business conferences—** Network with everyone while you are there. Ask questions, read articles, and learn as much as you can about the business side of the district. Based on what you learn, meet with your Assistant Superintendent of Business to discuss processes and procedures.
* **Contact Those in the Know.** Reach out to your mentors and rely on their guidance. Remember, they survived the superintendency!
* **Learn the Culture of Your District.** You can then balance your leadership with confidence and humor while questioning established practices. Eventually, my staff would preface their comments with, *'Here's another whiplash process you'll be interested in.'*
* **Trust your Gut.** If something doesn't sound right, get to the bottom of the issue. Believe in your instincts, even if you don't initially understand the specifics of the problem.
* **Don't Underestimate Your Abilities.** As a woman, this is your opportunity to lead with confidence, pride and strength. Let people know who you are and why you are the right person for the job. Celebrate all victories, make necessary changes using data, not perception, and remember to take your vitamins!

# VOICES OF POWER

Lead boldly, not perfectly: Courage matters more than perfection – step up even when the path is unclear.

## Chapter X

### TRUST YOUR GUT

### Inside a High-Stakes Superintendent Interview

#### Dr. Marilou Ryder

Have you ever found yourself at a career crossroads, torn between loyalty and opportunity? As a school superintendent in a thriving California district, I loved the board and the progress we were making. However, I faced a difficult reality: to secure a comfortable retirement, I needed a salary that reflected my experience and dedication. Having spent years in New York as an educator, I had only a few years vested in California's retirement system, where the final pension is calculated based on years of service and final salary. It was a pivotal moment that forced me to weigh my options: stay with a district I cherished or seek a new opportunity that could offer the financial security I desperately needed.

I received several raises over the course of four years, but the Board of Trustees informed me that they would not approve any further salary increases. Faced with this decision, I deliberated between two options: pursuing a position in a different district with a higher salary or remaining where I am and retiring with a modest annuity.

A headhunter reached out to me, claiming he had the 'perfect' district for my skills. The board reviewed my resume and expressed interest in learning more about me, specifically wanting to hire a woman for their superintendent position. This was great news.

Feeling optimistic, I told the headhunter, "I'm in," and spent the next month researching the school district and exploring real estate in the area. I was impressed by their initiatives for students and eager to join their team. The salary was very attractive and included a housing allowance and health insurance.

On the day of the interview, the headhunter told me, "This job is yours to lose. The board loves you and wants you as their new superintendent."

I interviewed on a Saturday, the day before Mother's Day, and it was my best interview ever. The board members were smiling and nodding in agreement with every word I said. I had never felt such assurance in a high-stakes interview environment before. I was on top of my game and felt confident.

As the interview concluded, everyone was smiling and shaking hands. "Thank you for coming today," the board president said. "We really like you."

The headhunter escorted me out of the conference room and added, "Be prepared for a final interview in about an hour. I'll call you on your phone when it's time. You did a great job, and I can tell this board wants you to be their next superintendent."

My husband, who always accompanies me to these excruciating events, suggested that we grab a cup of coffee and a light snack as it was approaching 4:00 PM. He had been waiting in the parking lot for over an hour. It was an excellent idea.

We found a charming little coffee shop a few miles from the district office. I wasn't in the mood for food, as I had a nervous feeling in my stomach. Eating was out of the question, but I thought a cup of coffee would give me the boost I needed for the final interview. I sat there, sipping coffee and waiting for the phone call.

My cell phone rang. "Get back to the district office as soon as possible; the board wants to hire you. They have a few questions before offering you a contract."

We jumped from our seats, paid the bill, which felt like it took forever and rushed back to our car. We were thrilled at the thought of moving to a new city. Both of us loved change and the prospect of retiring from a district with better retirement benefits.

Heading back to the district office, we took a wrong turn and found ourselves on a freeway instead of the intended route. Five miles passed, then ten. Where was the exit? After what felt like an eternity, perhaps 30 minutes, we finally spotted an off-ramp and made our way back to the district.

As someone who is meticulous about time, I was super anxious; nearly 45 minutes had passed since the headhunter's call. When we finally turned into the parking lot, I spotted him waving me toward the door. "Where have you been? This board is getting impatient. Let's go!"

Entering the conference room, I immediately sensed a shift in the atmosphere. The excitement that had filled the air was replaced by a palpable tension. Then I heard a statement that nearly stopped me in my tracks: "Let's get this done," exclaimed the Board President. "I have a lot to do at home to prepare for Mother's Day tomorrow."

Then it happened, something I would never have expected. The board's frustration escalated into outright insults and humiliation. "Why were you late? Don't you know we have things to do? If this is how you think of us, I don't know how we can proceed!"

"I'm sorry," I replied, my voice steady despite my rising anger. "We got lost and ended up on the freeway." But the negative attitude in the room remained unchanged. One board member abruptly asked to speak with the headhunter outside the conference room. He was gone for about ten minutes, leaving me to answer questions I had already addressed in the first interview, feeling the weight of their disapproval pressing down on me.

No one was smiling or looking at me. A sinking feeling coursed through my entire body. What am I doing here? These people are horrible and mean-spirited. The truth was glaringly evident: I had to get out of here.

When the headhunter finally returned, he managed to wrap up the interview with some forced pleasantries and handshakes. As he escorted me into the hotel lobby, he said, "Well, that didn't go well."

"I don't think I want to work for these people. If they can get this riled up over an honest mistake, what would they do in a board meeting if something didn't go their way?" The thought sent a chill down my spine.

"I understand," the headhunter replied, his tone sympathetic. "I knew they were challenging, but I didn't expect this level of hostility. I'll call you later in the week. Have a safe drive home."

I sat in my car for a moment, heart racing, not from nerves anymore, but from clarity. I had walked into that room wanting the job, truly believing it could be the next chapter I'd been working toward. However, as the interview unfolded, the truth also emerged.

The subtle jabs. The power plays. The unspoken expectation that I'd need to downplay who I am to fit in.

But that was never on the table.

I didn't leave that day defeated. I left proud. Proud that I could spot the difference between being chosen and being truly valued. The difference between chasing a title and stepping into purpose.

We often tell ourselves to push through, to prove ourselves, to accept what's offered. But sometimes, the most powerful move is choosing not to say yes.

While I didn't get the job, I got something better. I walked away with my integrity, and that, to me, is everything.

So here's the truth: even if you desperately want the position, you're still in control. An interview is a two-way street. Pay attention to how you're treated. Listen to your gut. If something feels off, trust yourself. You don't need all the answers to walk away with your dignity intact.

Because, in the end, turning down the wrong job is just as powerful as landing the right one.

**Legendary Insights**

* **Do Your Homework:** Dive deep into the organization you're considering joining. Speak with current employees about the district's culture. Do they lead with heart, or do they instill fear?
* **Trust your Gut:** If you feel uneasy during the interview, take a step back and try to assess the bigger picture. Remember, while they're interviewing you to see if you're the right fit for their organization, it works both ways. Look out for yourself and subtly evaluate whether they would be someone you'd actually want to work with.
* **Be Mindful of Communication Style:** Observe how the interviewers communicate with each other and with you. A respectful and constructive dialogue is a good sign, while negativity and hostility are major red flags.
* **Don't Rush the Process:** Take your time to reflect after an interview. Rushing into a decision can lead to misalignment with your professional goals and personal values.
* **Learn from Every Experience:** Each interview, whether successful or not, provides valuable insights. Reflect on your experiences to better prepare for future opportunities.

Change isn't a strategy — it's a survival skill.

## Chapter XI

### OPENING DOORS

### A Latina Superintendent's Journey in Collective Leadership

*Martha Martinez*

*"Life is all about moments. Leaders don't wait for them—they create them."*

~ Author Unknown

That moment came for me when I walked into the boardroom, not fully aware that what was about to happen would define how I approached leadership—not just in my district but across my entire community. I had been Superintendent of Salinas City Elementary School District (SCESD) for only a short time when I was asked a simple question. Could the Community Alliance for Safety and Peace (CASP) hold their monthly meetings in our boardroom?

It seemed like a small request. But saying yes would open far more than a meeting room. It would open a door—to visibility, connection, and a new kind of leadership. One not rooted in hierarchy or command but in compassion, collective power, and the belief that leadership is about creating space—especially for those too often left outside the door.

CASP was a powerhouse coalition led by city and county officials, law enforcement, nonprofits, and school leaders—all united around a single, powerful mission: protecting the children of our community. The group was traditional, male-dominated, and driven by titles—80% of the coalition were men, including the Mayor of Salinas and the Chair of the Monterey County Board of Supervisors. But that day, when I walked into the room, I saw something else: an opportunity—an opening.

That door didn't just open for a meeting. It opened for a woman of color to take her rightful place at the table in a space where voices like mine were too often absent. And once I was in, I made sure it stayed open for every woman coming after me.

It was the summer of 2015. The district was in a fragile place—still healing from the loss of a beloved former superintendent to cancer and the sudden resignation of the immediate past superintendent, weighed down by strained union relationships, and facing scrutiny from a community vigilante group demanding transparency. The Board was divided. Morale was low. Yet, beneath the surface, I found a committed team—people still driven by their belief in our mission. I realized then that leadership, especially as a woman of color, meant stepping fully into these complicated spaces. Not with force—but with a listening ear, open hands, and a heart ready to heal the broken parts of the district and build a greater sense of purpose and hope for all our stakeholders.

That first CASP meeting was transformational. The room was filled with the city's most influential leaders: the Mayor, the Chair of the Board of Supervisors, the CEOs of United Way, the Food Bank, nonprofit leaders, police chiefs, and advocates. I thought my role as the first Latina superintendent in that space would simply be a cordial welcome. What I learned, instead, is that my presence was not only welcome but also provided the opportunity for me to extend the invitation for others to join our efforts to redefine our district goals, create pathways to social, emotional well-being for our students, and find collaborative ways to build a stronger community who truly engaged with students and their families.

Leadership, I came to realize, isn't about standing out, commanding attention, or giving orders. It's about the power of invitation, creating spaces where others feel seen, valued, and empowered to thrive. And when I embraced that, everything changed.

From that one meeting, a ripple effect began. Our boardroom transformed into a hub for collective action, where walls came down and collaboration took root. What started as conversations grew into initiatives. Dreams became partnerships. Slowly, the impact spread beyond those four walls.

One of the most powerful partnerships to emerge was with Mayor Joe Gunter himself, who believed in the transformative power of early literacy in opening doors to our students' lifelong success. Together, we launched a city-wide bilingual early literacy initiative—one that would have a lasting impact on thousands of children in our city. We knew the data: 80% of our students came from low-income households, and more than half were English language learners. We knew about the "30-million-word gap"—the heartbreaking reality that children from low-income homes hear 30 million fewer words by age three than their wealthier peers. That gap sets the stage for a lifetime of educational disparities. We also knew we couldn't wait for mandated solutions. So, we created our own movement.

Through this initiative, families across the city of Salinas gained free access to an innovative bilingual early literacy app designed to empower parents as their children's first teachers. Training sessions were offered throughout the district, citywide banners graced the city and school entrances, and incentives were offered to teachers who used the application to build foundation skills. By the end of that first year, our youngest students had read an average of 50,000 words—each word a building block for their future.

For me, that initiative symbolized what's possible when leadership is rooted in connection and collective power. Where others might have led with mandates, I tried to lead by invitation. The results were amazing, and I realized that as a woman—especially a Latina superintendent—my leadership wouldn't always look like those who came before me. But that was the point.

These moments continued to build, leading us to milestone events like the city's and district's 150th Anniversary—Salinas' Sesquicentennial. Our district proudly hosted the Children's Area during the Founders Day celebration, creating a vibrant space that showcased the talents and spirit of our students and families. The arts came alive—art tents bursting with creativity, choirs lifting their voices, mariachi bands filling the air with music, and folklórico dancers bringing tradition to life. It was a celebration where children could see themselves reflected in the city's story. The one-day festival drew more than 10,000 attendees—a powerful reminder of how communities come together to honor their shared history and collective accomplishments. But this was more than a celebration; it was a reclamation. Our children were not just participants—they belonged in that history.

Then came one of the most powerful initiatives of my tenure—the March Against Bullying. Born from our shared commitment to student safety and well-being, this city-wide event united local law enforcement, city officials, our school board, and neighboring districts. By its third year, the March Against Bullying had become a living, breathing example of what collective power looks like.

By our third year, we had enlisted participation from our neighborhood High School, Salinas High School and Salinas' other elementary school district, Alisal Union School District. The event was unforgettable. High school bands and cheerleaders led the parade. The Alisal Union drumline's beats echoed through the streets. Each of our fourteen schools proudly carried banners they had designed—bright, creative declarations of our stand against bullying. We didn't just march—we made noise, we took space, and we showed every child watching that they mattered.

Nearly 2,500 students, parents, educators, and community members gathered that day at Salinas High School. An official proclamation from the city capped the event, but the real victory was the message: our community stands together. Not just once—but every year. We made this march an annual tradition, aligning each month's Positive Behavioral Interventions and Supports (PBIS) focus to culminate in this celebration of unity and resilience.

What grew from that foundation was a deep, systemic commitment to student wellness and safety. Our district adopted Multi-Tiered Systems of Support (MTSS) and expanded our Positive Behavioral Interventions and Supports (PBIS) work. We forged new partnerships—most notably with Harmony at Home—to bring additional social-emotional resources directly into our schools. This wasn't performative. It was essential. And it earned our district a Golden Bell Award—**Changing School Communities and Beyond** —a testament to the power of leading through collaboration and with the heart.

Throughout my journey, I was deeply humbled by the recognition our collective work received—powerful reminders of what becomes possible when a community comes together, centering children and equity at every turn. Together, we earned the distinction of being named a **Model Innovation City**. Our team was honored with another Golden Bell Award—**Heart for the Homeless**—for the systems and supports we built to serve our unhoused families. We were also recognized for our unwavering commitment to safety and peace, receiving the **CASP Founders Award** and being named the top leader in Monterey County.

Each of these honors reflected far more than individual leadership—they were a testament to the strength of shared purpose, collective action, and our community's deep commitment to those we serve. But awards were never the goal. They simply marked the doors we opened—together.

Still, what mattered most to me was the unseen impact—the quiet doors opening every day. I often thought about the female teachers and administrative leaders, as well as our young girls watching from the sidelines, wondering if there was space for them in leadership. I wanted every move I made to send a clear message: Yes. There is space not just for me but for you.

I cherished the conversations I shared with our female teacher leaders—women curious about their own leadership journeys. I told them what I wish someone had told me early on: *you don't have to start at the top*. I began as a paraprofessional, balancing work, family, and impossible choices. Every hard decision and every sacrifice propelled me forward—from teacher to principal, to director, assistant superintendent, and eventually, superintendent.

Along the way, I learned to search for brilliance in others—and I found it. My leadership team was full of gems: women who were not only highly skilled and experienced but also willing to take on the critical challenges we faced. My cabinet was predominantly female-driven, passionate, and fiercely loyal. They brought excellence to every table we sat at together.

I had never cried in my role as superintendent—until the day my assistant superintendent told me she was leaving for a position in higher education. She was my right hand. The loss felt overwhelming, but I knew I had to let her go so she could continue to soar. Today, she is the Chancellor of a community college system—a testament to her brilliance and strength.

Recently, at a Women's Leadership Conference, I heard a quote that stayed with me: *"Our role as women leaders is to find the brilliance in others and nurture them to reach their dreams."* That resonated deeply. I never set out to be a legend, but if my leadership opened doors for others—especially women of color—then maybe, just maybe, that's exactly what a legend does.

Five years. That's how long I served as Superintendent of SCESD. And in those five years, I learned that leadership isn't about having the loudest voice in the room. It's about knowing when to speak—and when to listen. It's about creating space for others, knowing that true power is shared.

I led differently—intentionally. Far from the command-and-control model traditionally associated with male leadership, I embraced a style grounded in empathy, connection, and collective action. In every decision, every partnership, every door opened, I asked: Who else can we bring with us?

Because ultimately, the doors we open aren't just for ourselves. They're for every woman and girl wondering if she belongs at the table. For every parent hoping for a better future. For every child learning that their words, their stories, and their dreams matter.

Looking back, I know this: I was at the right place, at the right time, for the right reasons. And if my leadership taught anyone that their voice matters—that they, too, can open doors—then that is the legacy I'm most proud of.

I didn't set out to be a legend. I set out to serve. But sometimes, maybe, legends are just women who dared to say yes—over and over again—until the world changed around them.

## LEGENDARY INSIGHTS

* **Leadership Begins with Human Connection**: True leadership is not rooted in authority but in building trust and meaningful relationships. I've learned that standing *with* others—listening, collaborating, and valuing diverse voices—creates the strongest foundation for leading lasting change.

* **Compassion is a Leader's Greatest Strength**: In moments of challenge, choosing compassion over command has opened doors to deeper understanding and stronger bonds. Whether supporting a struggling student or a staff member in crisis, leading with heart has always led us forward.

* **Recognition Reflects Impact, Not Ego**: Awards and honors have been moments of pride—but not because of the personal accolade. They serve as reminders that when we lead with integrity and purpose, the impact ripples across communities.

* **Breaking Barriers Creates Space for Others**: As a Latina superintendent, challenging traditional norms became necessary. By disrupting outdated systems, I've learned that leadership is about opening doors for those historically left outside—creating pathways for representation and equity.

* **The Power of 'We' is Greater than the Power of 'Me'**: Collective leadership is where true transformation happens. Working alongside educators, families, and community leaders reinforced that change is not carried

by one—it's carried by many, moving together with shared purpose.

* **Leadership is a Journey of Becoming**: Leadership is not a title or a destination but rather a continuous journey of reflection, learning, and growth. Every challenge faced, every lesson learned, shapes the leader I am becoming and fuels the vision for what is still possible.

# VOICES *OF* POWER

Decisions create momentum: Don't fear making the wrong choice – not deciding is the real setback.

## Chapter XII

## BUILT FROM THE GROUND UP

### Seven Lessons of Grit, Growth, and Leadership

*Dr. Cindy Petersen*

In my first twenty years of life, no one would have predicted that one day I'd become a superintendent-- and truly, I mean NO ONE – including myself. I sincerely hope your back story is smoother, brighter, and filled with more kindness than mine. And while my backstory and yours are interesting and important – those are stories for another day. Today, as I sit down at my computer and picture you – the reader – and what I most hope to share with you, I'd like to offer you some lessons learned from a leader *built from the ground up*.

No leader steps into their role fully formed, armed with perfected skills, innate attributes, or some kind of special leadership DNA. The very thought of this is laughable. In the early years of my leadership journey I would often look around me and think other leaders – and at the time they were predominantly male - had it all together and were the whole package while I felt somehow uniquely 'less than' and different.

Coming from a humble family where I was the first to pursue higher education, I believed, rightfully so, that I had already shattered expectations by earning a degree in mathematics, securing my credential, and stepping into the classroom as a high school math teacher. For all intents and purposes, that may have been the pinnacle of my career, and I very well could have stayed in that role and retired from it. I LOVED teaching and I LOVED my students and I felt very accomplished in light of exceeding everyone's expectations for me.

And then .... life in all its beautiful random, organic and chaotic way ... happened. I stumbled upon an opportunity to take a year's leave of absence from my district and pursue work in the young, volatile, and rapidly-growing California charter school movement. In that first year, my role expanded significantly – from teacher to teacher leadership and beyond. While there were multiple 'bumps' in the road of varying seismic power, I can say with conviction that that decision and that opportunity would launch me on an incredible leadership journey that would span three decades, open many doors and forge strengths I never knew I had.

At the time that I took my leave of absence, and I think it remains mostly true today, the school district path to the superintendency was lengthy and included a decade or more as a teacher, time as an assistant principal, more time as a principal, a transition to a district office role and then ultimately the superintendency. According to AASA (The School Superintendents Association), coaching activities have traditionally been an initial step toward administration, and, at least in the district where I taught, coaches (and administrators) were predominantly male.

My journey from teacher to superintendent didn't follow the traditional path, and honestly, as a single mother of four outside the inner circle of leadership, I often wondered if it would have ever happened for me in that setting. My journey certainly has some unique aspects.

For one thing, I progressed from teacher to mid-level management roles, then to site administration, district-level leadership, and ultimately to the superintendency, all much faster than the traditional district track. My superintendency was also somewhat unique - not many superintendents led and built their district across twenty years, from one school of about 300 students to nine schools of over 5000. I often say that I built a district from the ground up and that the journey has also built me as a leader. A twenty-year leadership journey of incredible organizational growth and development necessitated that my own leadership knowledge, competency, and execution also grow, change, and evolve to meet the moment.

Looking back, I can truly see what an incredible opportunity I was afforded. It wasn't easy. There were plenty of twists and turns, pain, and heartbreak, all of which were learning and growth opportunities. Ultimately, all of this eventually led to creating a personal and organizational mantra of feeling the fear and doing it anyway – 'Be Brave.'

Throughout my journey, I certainly learned to be brave, but I also picked up some valuable practical lessons. While there were many, seven stand out, and I share them with you in the hope that they will support your growth as a leader.

1. **So ... let's talk about YOU**

To lead others successfully, you must first know and understand yourself. Probably the first and foundational key is to identify and understand your core values. Knowing your core values allows you to lead in alignment with them, which creates clarity and integrity and instills trust in those you lead. Understanding your strengths and your areas for growth allows you to model the way for others in the organization. You can't simply rely on your own perceptions. There are various ways to gain insight. Leadership assessments and well-designed 360-degree evaluation instruments will provide you with greater insight – especially when they reveal discrepancies between how you think you are perceived and how you actually are perceived – ouch! Even the most reflective of leaders gain more self-awareness if they keep their hearts and minds open.

During my time in leadership, I utilized several of these instruments for both the organization and myself. Each instrument and each evaluation provided me with a new understanding –it wasn't always fun, but it helped me identify how I was getting in my own way. This willingness to be open and reflective to feedback is a true act of courage. When you can be honest, vulnerable, and authentic about your areas of growth, you create safety for others to be self-aware and grow. According to Abby Wambach in *The Wolfpack (2019)*[14], "The old way is to lead with invulnerability and enlist followers. The new way is to lead with full humanity – and cultivate a team of leaders."

The superintendency is a demanding role, and as women leaders, we often face additional challenges—biases, both conscious and unconscious, structural inequities, and societal pressures that dictate how we should dress, speak, and lead.

Often, as women leaders, we feel that to succeed, we need to work harder, be stronger, and more competent than our male counterparts. These obstacles can be frustrating, but they also offer opportunities to challenge norms and pave the way for future women leaders.

By standing firm in your values and embracing your unique leadership style unapologetically, you can redefine what strength and influence look like. One way to navigate the challenge of 'leading while female' is to build a network of mentors, allies, and supportive peers – particularly with other women leaders where we can provide and find support and guidance as we each navigate the challenges of leadership.

2. **So, you're the superintendent, and you're on your own now. But are you?**

Becoming a superintendent can feel like crossing into a great unknown, where the weight of responsibility is immense, and the expectation to have all the answers can be overwhelming. But despite the pressures of the role, you don't need to carry the burden alone—or wear an "S" on your chest like some kind of superhero. As a superintendent, your work and success are predicated on your team - how you invest in and grow them and the relationships you create with them. Asking for help, delegating, and relying on trusted team members are not signs of weakness—they are essential skills for empowered, sustainable leadership.

I truly believe that one of the most underrated yet powerful tools you can wield is relational capacity—the ability to build and maintain strong, meaningful connections. While deep relationships are invaluable, research shows that weak ties—those casual acquaintances and broader professional networks—are just as critical. In your role, you must form networks in the district, in the county office, at the state department of education, in educational associations, and in community politics – the more diverse these networks of weak ties are, the more they can provide fresh perspectives, access to resources, and connections that can lead to innovative solutions. In times of crisis or change, the ability to tap into these networks can make all the difference. Cultivating relationships with school leaders, community members, and even colleagues in different districts fosters a culture of support and shared wisdom, reinforcing that leadership is not meant to be a lonely endeavor.

3. **People Part 1: The opinion of others ...**

There will never be a shortage of opinions about your leadership. It helps to recognize that leadership, especially for women, often means navigating scrutiny that extends beyond decisions and into perceptions of confidence, ambition, and authority. While some feedback is constructive and worth considering, strong leaders develop discernment, knowing when to listen and whom to listen to. It is so important not to shrink or make yourself small in an attempt to please everyone – pleasing everyone is exhausting and ultimately impossible.

During my years as a superintendent, every 360-degree evaluation brought a flood of conflicting opinions: *"I love how often she is at my campus"* would be at odds with *"She needs to be on my campus more"*. The Board of Trustees evaluation would include scores of '*meets or exceeds expectations*' on all the items and then a board member would comment, "*It's too bad she has no leadership qualities*". The organizational-wide 360 reviews would also always yield a strange random comment or two: '*She should go to church.*' Or '*She should wear longer skirts*.' Or '*We should get paid more*' (which had nothing to do with the questions of course). The feedback and opinions expressed on 360s are most valuable when they represent a trend of responses – if a lot of people are noting that you don't delegate well, then that is something to reflect on (yes, that was one of my growth areas).

It's helpful to recognize that people's perceptions are often shaped by their own experiences, fears, and limitations—things that have very little to do with you. Instead of striving for universal approval, focus on your intention and impact, and remember that leadership requires courage, resilience, and the willingness to stand in your truth in alignment with your values.

4. **People Part 2: People stay and people leave [and it's not always about you …. And you will be okay].**

It's almost embarrassing to say this out loud but I struggled when people left the organization. Each departure felt like a personal failure as if their choice to move on reflected my shortcomings. It was an emotional weight I carried, one that made transitions harder than they needed to be. But with time, I came to see that people weren't leaving *me*—they were choosing what was best for *them*. Their decisions weren't judgments of my leadership but rather reflections of their own paths, needs, and growth. Learning this lesson didn't make goodbyes easy, but it softened the blow and shifted my perspective.

Instead of feeling hurt or betrayed, I wish I had celebrated more alongside those who were moving forward in their lives. Leadership isn't about holding on tightly—it's about guiding, supporting, and then letting go with grace when the time comes.

Ultimately, the biggest compliment I ever received as a leader was running into people who had once worked for me or alongside me and hearing them say that they were still using lessons they had learned from our time together in their new roles. Whether it was a mindset shift, a leadership approach, or a practical skill, knowing that something I had shared or modeled continued to shape their journey was incredibly fulfilling. It wasn't just about the work we did at the moment—it was about the lasting impact, the ripple effect of growth and empowerment that extended far beyond our time together.

5. **Culture is everything**

Tony Hsieh (2010)[15], the former entrepreneur and CEO of Zappos, is quoted as saying, *"For individuals, character is destiny. For organizations, culture is destiny."* Each of us probably has a story in our work history that involves a toxic culture – I know I do. Toxic cultures lead to employee dissatisfaction, disengagement and high turnover – no one wants that! (I didn't stay long in that organization.)

The development of organizational culture begins with identifying the current state, including the mission, vision, core values, recognitions, communication, written and unwritten norms, what is tolerated and what is not, and what we say versus what we do. This takes time, as well as the input and feedback of others and the willingness to listen with curiosity and without defensiveness.

As with most change – if change is in order – it is hard work. It will take time but it is so worth the effort. During my tenure as a superintendent, one school faced significant leadership challenges, including legal actions, substantial staff turnover, and declining morale and engagement. Starting from the ground up, we utilized surveys and feedback instruments to understand at least some of the concerns: unequal treatment, favoritism, 'good ole boys' mentality, and more. It needed a complete culture transformation to survive. It was hard, consistent, and intentional work with numerous forks in the road to transform, revise, and rebirth their identity and culture.

My role was to be consistent and intentional, and as the superintendent, to speak it, live it, walk it, and create structures, systems, and rituals to keep it strong. I also had to confront anything that might pull them back towards the toxicity of the past, including at one point when I had to replace the principal and a few others. Just to reiterate, I don't want to imply it's easy – but it's critical. Peter Drucker's (2011)[16] famous quote, *"Culture eats strategy for breakfast,"* speaks to the power of culture in shaping success.

When culture becomes ingrained in the way people think and work, it functions much like Jim Collins' (2001)[17] *flywheel effect* in *Good to Great*—where small, intentional efforts compound over time, generating powerful forward momentum. Just like at the school I was working on turning around – it takes a lot of consistent and intentional work to birth and embed a great culture. Once that culture is strong and has become the identity, the momentum will continue to build and maintain itself with less effort than during the transformation itself. Building a cohesive and thriving district culture is a long journey, requiring persistence and countless steps before real shifts become evident. Yet, once achieved, the impact is transformational.

6. **Not only can you be inspirational and motivational and find ways to spark energy ... You must!**

As I learned to lead – and the early years were rough for sure – I put my head down and just tried to get the work done. I suppose I was hoping that working hard and being competent would inspire 'followership'. Ultimately, it was Bethany Rosebrock of the Flippen Group who gave me permission to be inspirational. She sat down with me over lunch, and I shared my hopes and dreams for the organization. In particular, we discussed my vision and thoughts on our upcoming administrators' retreat. It wasn't as if part of me didn't know that inspiration was necessary and important, but hearing her make it clear that **I** could **BE** inspirational and that the admin team and organization NEEDED me to be inspirational – that was a whole new world.

I realized that inspiration isn't just a nice-to-have; it's a responsibility, and it was **MY** responsibility. People need energy, encouragement, and reminders of what is possible, especially during challenging times. That's not just for them; it's for you, too. Because when you align your actions with your deepest reasons for doing what you do, you don't just inspire— you ignite.

This truth became more evident than ever as we led our organizations through the COVID-19 Pandemic. The breadth and depth of the challenges facing everyone made the world feel heavy, and hope was hard to find. As a leader at this time, I clearly didn't think it was enough to assume people knew they were cared for; they needed to *see* it, *hear* it, and *feel* it—continually and consistently.

Whether through a message, a conversation, or simply showing up with unwavering belief in our ability to do what had to be done each day to survive and take care of our students, families, and ourselves – we were called to be vulnerable, strong, and brave, and our presence mattered more than ever. Inspiration isn't a one-time act; it's a daily practice. The more people see and hear you bringing light, the more they'll believe they can do the same. And when we all bring our light – it's amazing how much brighter it shines.

7. **I know we've talked a lot about you – but remember that ultimately, It's not about You – It's about them.**

While much of what I've discussed here has focused on you as the leader, we must continually and intentionally keep our focus on the people we serve – our employees, students, families, and community. The true measure of your leadership is how much potential you unlock in others. When you focus on empowering your team—whether it's educators, staff, or students—you create an environment where they can thrive. Your greatest success isn't in personal accolades but in watching those around you grow, innovate, and succeed because of the foundation you've helped build.

As Frei and Morriss (2020)[18] emphasize in their book *Unleashed,* leadership is about the lasting impact of your presence and ensuring that your influence continues even when you are not there. The hallmark of leadership is not in making yourself indispensable but in how effectively you prepare others to lead in their own right. By fostering confidence, autonomy, and a shared vision, you create a culture where success is not reliant on one person but is instead deeply embedded in the organization. The legacy you leave behind will not be about how much you accomplished but about how many people you empowered to reach their fullest potential and what you created together.

These seven insights are, of course, not all that I learned in my over twenty years as a superintendent. There were small lessons, mid-sized lessons and large lessons – mostly forged from challenges, difficult circumstances, missteps, and, yes, failures. Ultimately, every day of your superintendency presents you with a plethora of challenges. You mostly don't get to know or choose your challenges but do you know what you can control? Your actions. Each day, you can get up, lead, and live with heart, in alignment with your core values, in concert with your district's vision, and in service of your students and community - and model that for everyone in the district.

Leadership is a journey and one that must be built from the ground up. Like any quality building project, your leadership will be built over time and with intention. You start by building a strong foundation of knowing who you are and what you stand for. Once you have a strong foundation, you can develop your grit, resilience, and leadership strength by continually learning from your challenges and failures. Recognize where you are on the journey and celebrate the lessons you've already learned. Hopefully, some of the lessons I've shared will also propel you as you build your leadership from the ground up.

## LEGENDARY INSIGHTS

* **True leadership is built over time, not bestowed instantly.** Remember - no one steps into a leadership role fully formed! Your leadership journey requires growth, learning, and the willingness to embrace the challenges.

*"Choose courage over comfort by vitally engaging with new opportunities to learn and grow." Susan David (2022)[19].*

* **Self-awareness is the bedrock of effective leadership.** It is key to leadership and life to identify and live within your core values. Self-awareness depends on self-reflection, but it also relies on being open to the feedback of others, who can provide valuable insights to support you in leading with integrity, building trust, and modeling the way for others to grow.

*"Leadership is a continuous journey of growth, self-awareness, and purpose. Every challenge is a chance to inspire and learn, both about ourselves and about guiding others." Dr. Derrick Love (2022)[20]*

* **Relational capacity is an underappreciated superpower.** You cannot function as an island; leadership is not a solitary journey. Cultivating strong relationships and diverse networks of support is critical to navigating challenges and the synergy that results leads to innovative solutions.

*"We interact with people every day, and we live our lives in the context of our relationships. This includes our work lives. ... Relationships trump everything else." Frank Molinario (2018).*[21]

* **The opinions of others are inevitable but not definitive.** Do listen to everything with an open heart and mind. Then, discernment should be used regarding the value and validity of the feedback as well as the intent of the person giving it. Surround yourself with trusted truth-tellers to contest, confirm or support the feedback provided.

*"The desire for approval is deeply ingrained in human nature. We want to be liked, respected, and validated. But when this need becomes a driving force, it can undermine your effectiveness as a leader." Moe Nawaz (2024).*[22]

* **Leadership is about empowering others, not about you.** While leadership and power are part of the journey, pairing them with an unchecked ego is a recipe for failure—not success. It's a human flaw, but not an unavoidable one. The true measure – and the heart of leadership is how well you unlock potential in others by creating an environment where your team can thrive and succeed independently.

*"Leadership, at its core, isn't about you. Instead, it's about how effective you are at empowering other people and unleashing their full potential." Morris and Frei (2020).*[23]

* **Inspiration is a leader's daily responsibility.** The work matters – you matter – they matter! It's not enough to hope for inspiration to emerge; you must actively provide energy, encouragement, and hope, especially in challenging times. That's not just for them; it's for you, too! Because when you align your actions with your deepest reasons for doing what you do, you don't just inspire—you ignite.

*"It's not about where people work that should serve as the focus of your leadership. The question you should be asking yourself is what are you doing to create a sense of purpose within your organization?" Tanveer Naseer (2020).*[24]

* **Culture shapes the destiny of an organization.** Culture, whether positive or negative, is a key driver and multiplier of an organization's work. Uncovering or discovering your culture – spoken and unvoiced – and then the work of creating a positive organizational culture takes time and intentionality, but once ingrained, it becomes a propelling force for sustained success and transformation.

*"Organizational cultures are created by leaders, and one of the decisive functions of leadership may well be the creation, the management, and – if and when that may become necessary – the destruction of culture." Edgar Schein (2010).*[25]

Trust isn't given — it's earned in the quiet moments.

## Chapter XIII

### WHEN IT'S TIME TO LEAVE

*Dr. Myrna Rivera Côté*

Ask any experienced superintendent the question, "How do you know when it's time to leave a superintendent position?" and the answer will probably be, "When you can no longer count to three." As simple as that may sound, the truth is that when you are a superintendent with a five-member Board of Trustees, being able to count on three of those Board members for support is critical to your longevity. You may, however, find yourself in a situation where you can currently count to three: you love the school district, the community is supportive, and the schools are thriving, but there is an upcoming Board of Trustees election. Call it woman's intuition or simply the rumbling of my Bronx gut, but I sensed that the upcoming Board election would bring significant changes to the status quo.

I found myself in this dubious position after serving as superintendent for five years in a middle-sized district in Los Angeles County. During those five years, our students improved academically, our community rallied to pass a Bond Measure, we dramatically increased our educational partners' support, and I could go on and on. We had all worked very hard, and we were extremely proud of our accomplishments.

The Board of Trustees election was approaching, and three long-standing Board members were not running for reelection. Bringing on new Board members is always a challenge for superintendents as the importance of having a cohesive and collaborative Board of Trustees is mandatory for a successful school district. My administrative staff and I met with each candidate individually and attended the candidate forums. We provided as much district information as we could to ensure an informed candidate pool. We waited for the election results apprehensively, knowing that a change of three members would present a significant challenge.

My team and I did everything possible to welcome and integrate the new members of the Board of Trustees. I toured the schools with them, had lunch with the new Board President, reviewed the specifics of the Brown Act with them, and invited them to school events, among other things. I also hired consultants to do a workshop for them on important Board protocols. The workshop began well. However, one hour into a three-hour workshop, two of the new members, including the new Board President, got up and left. They stated that they did not need this information and that it was a waste of their time. The consultants were shocked but continued their presentation for the remaining Board member and me. After the workshop was over, I received my first warning from an experienced outsider. He said, "You won't be able to successfully work with this Board. It's time for you to move on."

As the school year progressed, the challenges presented by this new Board became increasingly apparent to school district personnel and the community. Board meetings became entertainment venues as the Board questioned and often ridiculed every item on the agenda. Comments made by Board members at the annual Founders Day celebration were rude and disgraceful to the attendees. Board meetings held in large forums during budget presentations featured a Board member holding up a giant-sized calculator that he used to challenge the budget numbers. As the community watched closely, my team and I graciously responded to the Board's questions. We accepted the results of their votes, which included cutting critical positions and funding allocations that had not been recommended by staff. I had been advised early in my administrative career to "never let them see you sweat." So, I remained cordial and professional as I endured each Board meeting with staff's and community members' eyes on my every move.

Soon after the budget meetings ended, I attended a City Council meeting to meet the newly elected City Council members. It was a very large and celebratory gathering, also honoring the outgoing City Council members. After the meeting ended, I was walking back to my office when a highly respected City Council member began walking beside me. After some pleasant conversation, he calmly asked me, "Why are you still here? You are a good superintendent and should be working with a School Board that works with, not against, you." I thanked him for his concern and support, but I was shocked to hear his words. I knew that if he felt this way, many others must have felt the same way. I knew I had to make a difficult decision—whether to leave a district I loved, knowing I could no longer thrive there. I had become the center of the storm, and with my contract renewal coming up in a few months, I knew I had no choice but to leave.

In many of the stories in this book, you've read of the importance of staying true to yourself, upholding your morals, trusting your gut and maintaining your integrity. I realized that I could no longer do these things in this district. Every iota of the core of my being was challenged on a daily basis. I was the focal point rather than the district, the students, or the victories we had won. I could not let this situation continue. At my final principal's meeting of the year, I told them that I was leaving because staying true to yourself is crucial in leadership, and I wanted them to always remember that.

I was able to secure a new superintendency fairly easily through valuable contacts I had made over the years. Once I finalized my new contract, I called each Board member to inform them that I had a new Superintendent position and would be leaving the district at the end of June. I made each call after 5:00 p.m. on the Friday before Memorial Day weekend. I knew this information would spread like wildfire throughout the community and I needed the long weekend away to deal with the fallout. There were many tears and hugs as I packed up my office that June. However, this strong, principled woman was proud to stand by her decision to move on when she knew it was the right time to do so.

## LEGENDARY INSIGHTS

* **The Power of Timing:** Leadership shines brightest when it's grounded in integrity. Sometimes, the most courageous decision is knowing when it's time to move on.

* **Respect Your Worth:** Even when others diminish your contributions or attempt to undermine your leadership, remember your accomplishments and the impact you have made. You deserve to work with people who recognize and support your efforts.

* **Trust Your Gut and Your Exit Strategy:** Intuition is a powerful leadership tool. When your internal compass signals that trouble is ahead, listen. And when you choose to exit, do so with grace, professionalism, and a well-timed plan.

* **Lead with Integrity, Leave with Dignity:** A principled leader knows that staying true to one's values may sometimes mean stepping away. The legacy you leave behind is shaped not just by your success but by how you exit when leadership conditions change.

## VOICES OF POWER

Stand in your power: Confidence isn't arrogance – it's knowing your value and not being afraid to show it.

## Chapter XIV

## BOLD ENOUGH TO BELIEVE

*Dr. Carol Riley*

Aloha! My name is Dr. Carol Riley, and I've spent a lifetime in education. I was a teacher, a principal (four times over), an assistant superintendent, and a superintendent. I've lived in Hawaii for many years now, but my story actually begins in California, where I served as a school district superintendent. Each role I held brought its challenges, but at the heart of it all, I was always a teacher. I simply taught different groups of students, sometimes children, sometimes teachers, staff, or an entire community.

After serving as superintendent for four years, I took a long, hard look at our schools. The challenges were clear: aging facilities, outdated classrooms, and growing enrollment. It was time to act. I knew we needed change, but I also understood that change required community-wide effort. It couldn't be just my plan—it had to be our plan. And so, I began asking questions: *What was the condition of our buildings? Could they accommodate future students? Did they support the needs of modern education?* What questions hadn't I even thought of yet?

As I reflected on these challenges, I arrived at a bold idea: we needed to pass a school bond. I knew this was an audacious idea. At the time, no school bond had ever been passed in Orange County, California. I turned to my colleagues and friends for their thoughts, and the response was unanimous: *Carol, this is a bad idea. You won't win.*

But I couldn't let go of the thought: *If not now, when?*

The task ahead was daunting. A bond measure would require educating and rallying an entire community, many of whom didn't have children in our schools or understand the depth of our needs. I began by reaching out to our Board of Education. From there, I moved on to our administrators, teachers, and staff. I met with PTAs, church groups, service clubs like the Lions Club and Boys and Girls Club, and anyone who would listen.

Together, we began creating a vision. We hired a school planner and an architect to assist us in developing a Facilities Master Plan. This was about the future. The plan outlined how we could repair leaky roofs, update aging plumbing and electrical systems, and replace outdated temporary classrooms with permanent ones. However, we also knew that this effort had to be about more than just buildings. It had to be about community trust and collaboration.

To move forward, we established committees, held community meetings, and gathered input from every corner of the district. It took time and plenty of patience to get everyone on the same page. But I believed in the power of teaching. This time, the lesson was for our entire community: *Our schools matter. Our kids matter. And this bond can change everything.*

A major hurdle remained: the bond measure had to be approved by local voters, many of whom were taxpayers without children in our schools. Would they see the value? Would they understand the needs of the next generation? I knew the answer lay in trust. If we built strong relationships, we could overcome any doubt.

Trust, I've learned, is the foundation of all great leadership. Whether you're a teacher in a classroom, a principal leading a school, or a superintendent guiding an entire district, trust creates safety. And safety allows people to learn, grow, and take risks. I reminded myself often that the best leaders are not know-it-alls. They are humble. They listen, they learn, and they make others feel seen and heard.

And so, we pressed on. Through open conversations, careful planning, and a relentless focus on our shared purpose, we earned the community's support.

I will never forget the night of the bond vote. Sitting in a room full of nervous anticipation, we watched the results roll in. Against all odds, the bond passed. We did it! The news surprised many, including some who doubted we could ever succeed. However, we demonstrated to them what trust, vision, and collective effort can achieve.

That victory didn't stop with us. Inspired by our success, other districts followed suit. School bonds began passing across the county, transforming schools and communities for the better.

Looking back, I now see that taking the step forward with the bond was both a professional and personal risk. As a woman in leadership, I often felt the weight of having to prove myself in ways my male counterparts didn't. Some people questioned the idea, but others quietly questioned *me*. I could sense the doubt that hung in the air—not just about the bond's chances, but about whether I had what it took to pull it off. That's a challenge many women leaders face: the burden of having to be twice as prepared, twice as measured, and still bold enough to lead through resistance. I kept going—not to prove them wrong, but to prove our students right. They deserved someone who wouldn't back down.

And no matter what title I held, I was still teaching—just with a bigger classroom and a deeper lesson.

## LEGENDARY INSIGHTS

* **Dream Big:** Don't be afraid to imagine what hasn't been done yet. Bold ideas often start with a quiet thought—and grow through courage, collaboration, and commitment. Even if others doubt you, stay rooted in your purpose. Big dreams lead to lasting change when you believe in your vision and invite others to share it with you.
* **Complete your homework.** Take a thorough look at the schools. Be honest. Ask others for their opinions. A bunch of heads are better than one.
* **Consider opportunities.** As you begin the process, consider your accomplishments. Expand your thinking. Think "out of the box". Know that possibilities are endless.
* **Celebrate learning.** New opportunities provide expanded learning. Remember the importance of being professional and staying positive. Flexibility is key.
* **Trust and Humility Matter:** The best leaders create spaces where people feel heard, valued, and safe.

# LEGACY TRUTHS

Your success is the foundation for someone else's starting point.

# REFERENCES

## Introduction

1 Blount, J. M. (1998). *Destined to rule the schools: Women and the superintendency, 1873–1995.* State University of New York Press.
2 American Association of School Administrators. (2025, April 1). AASA releases 2024–25 superintendent salary & benefits study. https://www.aasa.org/news-media/news/2025/04/01/aasa-releases-2024-25-superintendent-salary-benefits-study
3 National Center for Education Statistics. (2023). Characteristics of public school teachers (Condition of Education 2023). U.S. Department of Education. https://nces.ed.gov/programs/coe/pdf/2023/clr_508.pdf

## The Days are Long but the Years are Short

4 Blanchard, K., & Bowles, S. (2001). *High five! The magic of working together.* William Morrow.
5 Brown, B. (2018). *Dare to lead: Brave work. Tough conversations. Whole hearts.* Random House.
   Some concepts included came from or were built on the following resource: leanin.org/tips/workplace-ally#!

## Grace Under Fire

6 **ILO Group.** (2022). *The superintendent research project: December 2022 update.* [Report]. https://www.ilogroup.com/wp-content/uploads/2022/12/The-Superintendent-Research-Project_Dec-2022-Update.pdf
7 Keillor, G. (1995). *We are still married: Stories & letters.* Penguin Books.

## The Day the Dead Guy Drove to School

8  American Association of School Administrators. (2025). *Women in the superintendency: Leadership equity and representation.* AASA.

9  Arriaga, T. T., Stanley, S. L., & Lindsey, D. B. (2020). *Leading while female: A culturally proficient response for gender equity.* Thousand Oaks, CA: Corwin.

10  California Department of Education. (2020, May 13). *SSPI Thurmond announces 2019–20 enrollment data* [Press release]. https://www.cde.ca.gov/nr/ne/yr20/yr20rel23.aspCalifornia Department of Education

11  Chiefs for Change. (2019). Breaking through: Shattering the glass ceiling for women leaders. Retrieved from https://chiefsforchange.org/wp-content/uploads/2019/04/CFC-WomenLeaders-Final-April-23-2019.pdf

12  Robinson, K., Shakeshaft, C., Grogan, M., & Newcomb, W. S. (2017). Necessary but not sufficient: The continuing inequality between men and women in educational leadership, findings from the American Association of School Administrators mid-decade survey. Frontiers in Education, 2, 12.

13  Sanchez-Hucles, J. V., & Davis, D. D. (2010). Women and women of color in leadership: Complexity, identity, and intersectionality. American Psychologist, 65(3), 171–181. https://doi.org/10.1037/a0017459

## Built from the Ground Up

14  Wambach, A. (2019). *Wolfpack: How to come together, unleash our power, and change the game.* Celadon Books.

15  Hsieh, T. (2010). *Delivering happiness: A path to profits, passion, and purpose.* Business Plus.

16  Katzenbach, J. R., & Harshak, A. (2011). *Cultural change*

*that sticks*. Harvard Business Review. https://hbr.org/2011/07/cultural-change-that-sticks

17    Collins, J. (2001). *Good to great: Why some companies make the leap... and others don't*. HarperBusiness.

18    Frei, F., & Morriss, A. (2020). *Unleashed: The unapologetic leader's guide to empowering everyone around you*. Harvard Business Review Press.

19    David, S. (2022, August 17). *The emotional agility manifesto*. SusanDavid.com. https://www.susandavid.com/newsletter/the-emotional-agility-manifesto/

20    Love, D. (2022). *Self-Awareness in Leadership: Why the Best Leaders First Examine and Lead Themselves*. Kharis Publishing

21    Molinaro, F. (2018, October 24). In leadership, relationships matter most. Forbes. https://www.forbes.com/councils/forbeshumanresourcescouncil/2018/10/24/in-leadership-relationships-matter-most/

22    Nawaz, M. (2024, November 27). *Breaking free – Why leaders must stop seeking approval from the wrong people*. Medium. https://medium.com/@moenawaz/breaking-free-why-leaders-must-stop-seeking-approval-from-the-wrong-people-666e8bc41229

23    Frei, F., & Morriss, A. (2020). *Unleashed: The unapologetic leader's guide to empowering everyone around you*. Harvard Business Review Press.

24    Naseer, T. (2020, March 3). *Why now is the time for leaders to make purpose-led work their top priority*. TanveerNaseer.com. https://tanveernaseer.com/why-purpose-led-work-is-critical-for-organizational-success/

25    Schein, E. H. (2010). *Organizational culture and leadership* (4th ed.). Jossey-Bass.

# VOICES *OF* POWER

Don't hold yourself back – you're more ready than you think.

## About the Authors

**MYRNA RIVERA CÔTÉ, ED.D.**, has dedicated her life to improving educational opportunities for students of all ages. Starting as a Kindergarten teacher's aide, she rose through the teaching and administrative ranks of public schools, eventually serving as the first female Deputy Superintendent in a large urban school system. After completing her Doctorate in Education at USC, she broke the glass ceiling by serving as Superintendent in four school districts in Southern California. Upon retirement, she was hired by Brandman University (now UMass Global), where she taught Educational and Organizational Leadership to doctoral students. Additionally, she served as a Cohort Mentor in the doctoral program, guiding and challenging numerous students on their leadership journeys. A fierce advocate for female leadership, Dr. Côté's proudest accomplishments are now reflected in the former female students and staff members who now fill the roles she once held as Superintendent.

**LILLIAN MALDONADO FRENCH, ED.D.**, is the recently retired Superintendent of the Mountain View School District in El Monte, California. She has over 35 years of experience in public education, including roles as a Bilingual Teacher, Curriculum Specialist, Principal, and Director of Curriculum and Staff Development, as well as more than 15 years of experience as Superintendent in two urban school districts.

She received her B.A. in Linguistics from the University of California, Irvine, an M.S. in Educational Administration from California State University, Fullerton, and her doctorate in Organizational Leadership from Brandman University. Dr. French's diversified and successful professional experience has led to her expertise in coaching school boards and superintendents, addressing the needs of English Learners, developing research-based instructional programs, and maintaining effective family and community engagement through consensus-building and collaboration. Dr. French was named Superintendent of the Year for Los Angeles County. Since retiring, Dr. French has served as an adjunct professor, dissertation committee member, and as Board of Director of an extended learning nonprofit organization.

**LISBETH JOHNSON, ED.D.,** is a ground-breaking coach who develops emerging leaders. Lisbeth is recognized for her ability to build highly productive teams in organizations that may find themselves immersed in pre-existing chaos. Intuitive and innovative, she often paves the way for creating the conditions for group transformation. Dr. Johnson has co-authored Ice Age Schools, a book about twenty-first-century learning. She is a passionate advocate for diverse student populations. Serving on multiple public charter and private school boards, she is an inspiring promoter for inner-city youth, helping them rise above their circumstances. In her early career, she was voted among the top ten Principals in San Diego County to admire. Dr. Johnson has continued to receive numerous honors, including former Superintendent, Administrator of the Year for ACSA's Region 18, the Santee Chamber of Commerce President's Award and the California Legislative Assembly's Recognition for her instructional achievements.

**LINDA KIMBLE, ED.D.,** was one of the very few female leaders at the beginning of her sixteen-year tenure as Superintendent of Schools. She served in five unique school districts, from rural to urban and small to large. Dr. Kimble was honored as an Association of California School Administrators Superintendent of the Year, Region 14. Dr. Kimble, the author of two books, has written two compendiums of guidance for award-winning principals, superintendents, and emerging instructional leaders who strive to make a difference in student achievement. Dr. Kimble has served as chair and committee member for the doctoral programs at the University of Massachusetts Global and the University of La Verne.

**MARTHA L. MARTINEZ** is a retired Superintendent with over 25 years of leadership experience in California's K-12 public education system. Most recently, she served as Co-Executive Director of the California Association of Latino Superintendents and Administrators (CALSA), supporting over 1,000 educational leaders statewide. She held senior roles at school, district, and county levels—most notably as

Superintendent of Salinas City Elementary, where she led efforts to advance equity, close achievement gaps, and build strong community partnerships. Her previous roles include Assistant Superintendent for North Monterey County Unified and Senior Director at the Santa Clara County Office of Education, impacting over 265,000 students across 32 districts. A tireless advocate for educational equity, Martinez has collaborated with state agencies, led large-scale professional development initiatives, and driven reforms that have improved student outcomes. Her work has earned numerous honors, including the ACSA Region 10 Ferd Kiesel Award, CALSA and ACSA Superintendent of the Year, and multiple legislative proclamations. She holds a Master's in Organization and Leadership from the University of San Francisco, a Bachelor's in Child Development from San Jose State University, and professional credentials in teaching and administration. Her mission remains to empower educators, uplift Latino leadership, and transform public education.

**CINDY PETERSEN, ED.D.,** was 2019 ACSA's Exemplary Woman in Education as well as ACSA Region 3's Outstanding Woman Leader for 2020. In 2023, she was one of Comstock magazine's Women in Leadership honorees. Dr. Petersen has been a leader in public education for over 35 years, serving as Superintendent/C.E.O. of Gateway Community Charters. She has been an adjunct professor for Brandman University and the UMass Global doctorate programs for over a decade.

She is currently the CEO and Senior Leadership Consultant of Courageous Leadership Coaching and Consulting.

**CAROL RILEY, ED.D.,** is a lifelong educator with a passion for teaching and learning. Her journey began as a child, teaching her friends to swim, and continued in high school, where she guided others as a cheerleading coach. Over the years, Carol has held diverse roles in education, including elementary, middle, and high school teacher, university instructor, principal (four times), and Superintendent. Her career is marked by a relentless pursuit of new challenges and a deep love for inspiring others through education. Carol earned her Bachelor's degree from Central Missouri State University, her Master's from the University of Missouri, and her Doctorate from La Verne University. She considers herself blessed to have a supportive husband, the world's best puppy, and so many wonderful friends who enrich her life.

**MARILOU RYDER, ED.D.,** is a professor of higher education and recognized authority on women's leadership. With a decade leading large school districts as a Superintendent, she understands firsthand the ever-changing landscape of women in the workplace. An author of twelve books, her Amazon bestsellers blend interviews and research to empower women to harness their personal power for confidence and influence. As the Program Chair for the doctoral program at UMass Global, she champions self-empowerment through evidence-based techniques, igniting others to face life's challenges with courage. Dr. Ryder's captivating speaking engagements, infused with humor, leave audiences inspired. Her accolades include being named a Top Ten Businesswoman, California Administrator of the Year, and Orange County Professor of the Year, cementing her reputation as a dynamic leader in empowerment.

**PATRICIA CLARK WHITE, ED.D.,** is a distinguished educational leader with significant experience in both K12 and higher education. Dr. White has served in various capacities, including teacher, school leader, district administrator, university professor, associate dean, and dean. She spent a remarkable twenty-one years as Superintendent, leading three diverse districts in Southern California. She is well-known for her exceptional leadership skills and depth of knowledge in futures-based planning, organizational development, program evaluation, program accountability, finding common ground, and leveraging the political environment to deliver the vision. Her collaborative style with faculty and students is vision- and values-driven, emphasizing both support and accountability. Honored by her colleagues at the state, regional, and local levels, she has been named Superintendent of the Year by the California School Leadership Academy, Professor of the Year by ACSA Region 17, Buena Park Citizen of the Year, Woman of the Year by a number of organizations, and Mentor Hall of Fame by Southern Counties Women in Educational

Management. She is a presenter and author on many significant topics in 21st-century educational and organizational systems, and the book for which she served as lead author, *Political Intelligence*, is in its second edition.

**MARYLOU K. WILSON, ED.D.,** began her career in the public school system as a classified employee serving as a teacher's aide. Soon after starting her assignment, her teacher broke her ankle, and Marylou was put in charge of the classroom for six weeks. The substitute teacher provided her with support in the classroom. Marylou found her calling in education and never looked back. As an accomplished aide, classroom teacher, site administrator, and central office administrator, she transitioned into the superintendency in the last decade of her career. During that time, she also worked in higher education as a doctoral coach, instructor, and mentor. For over 35 years, Marylou has been recognized for her unwavering commitment to prioritizing students in all decisions, her exceptional leadership, and her ability to guide a community through challenges and achieve success. She is also known for her integrity, willingness to ask hard questions, and readiness to take the necessary risks to serve the student and staff community.

www.ingramcontent.com/pod-product-compliance
Lightning Source LLC
LaVergne TN
LVHW051833080426
835512LV00018B/2860